C000045552

Shakespeare and Cultural Materialist Theory

Shakespeare and Cultural Materialist Theory

Christopher Marlow

THE ARDEN SHAKESPEARE
LONDON • NEW YORK • OXFORD • NEW DELHI • SYDNEY

THE ARDEN SHAKESPEARE
Bloomsbury Publishing Plc
50 Bedford Square, London, WC1B 3DP, UK
1385 Broadway, New York, NY 10018, USA

BLOOMSBURY, THE ARDEN SHAKESPEARE and the Arden Shakespeare logo
are trademarks of Bloomsbury Publishing Plc

First published in 2017
Paperback edition printed 2019

Copyright © Christopher Marlow, 2017

Christopher Marlow has asserted his right under the Copyright,
Designs and Patents Act, 1988, to be identified as author of this work.

For legal purposes the Acknowledgements on p. vii constitute
an extension of this copyright page.

Series design by Sutchinda Rangsi Thompson
Cover image: X-ray image of Phalaenopsis Orchid head on white
background © Nick Veasy/Getty Images

All rights reserved. No part of this publication may be reproduced or
transmitted in any form or by any means, electronic or mechanical,
including photocopying, recording, or any information storage or retrieval
system, without prior permission in writing from the publishers.

Bloomsbury Publishing Plc does not have any control over, or responsibility for,
any third-party websites referred to or in this book. All internet addresses
given in this book were correct at the time of going to press. The author and
publisher regret any inconvenience caused if addresses have changed or sites
have ceased to exist, but can accept no responsibility for any such changes.

A catalogue record for this book is available from the British Library.

A catalog record for this book is available from the Library of Congress.

ISBN: HB: 978-1-4725-7296-7
PB: 978-1-4725-7293-6
ePDF: 978-1-4725-7294-3
eBook: 978-1-4725-7295-0

Series: Shakespeare and Theory

Typeset by Fakenham Prepress Solutions, Fakenham, Norfolk NR21 8NN

To find out more about our authors and books visit
www.bloomsbury.com and sign up for our newsletters.

For Annabelle

CONTENTS

SERIES EDITOR'S PREFACE

'Asking questions about literary texts – that's literary criticism. Asking "Which questions shall we ask about literary texts?" – that's literary theory.' So goes my explanation of the current state of English studies, and Shakespeare studies, in my never-ending attempt to demystify, and simplify, theory for students in my classrooms. Another way to put it is that theory is a systematic account of the nature of literature, the act of writing, and the act of reading.

One of the primary responsibilities of any academic discipline – whether in the natural sciences, the social sciences, or the humanities – is to examine its methodologies and tools of analysis. Particularly at a time of great theoretical ferment, such as that which has characterized English studies, and Shakespeare studies, in recent years, it is incumbent upon scholars in a given discipline to provide such reflection and analysis. We all construct meanings in Shakespeare's texts and culture. Shouldering responsibility for our active role in constructing meanings in literary texts, moreover, constitutes a theoretical stance. To the extent that we examine our own critical premises and operations, that theoretical stance requires reflection on our part. It requires honesty, as well. It is thereby a fundamentally radical act. All critical analysis puts into practice a particular set of theoretical premises. Theory occurs from a particular standpoint. There is no critical practice that is somehow devoid of theory. There is no critical practice that is not implicated in theory. A common-sense, transparent encounter with any text is thereby impossible. Indeed, to the extent that theory requires us to question anew that with which we thought we were familiar, that which we thought we understood, theory constitutes a critique of common sense.

Since the advent of postmodernism, the discipline of English studies has undergone a seismic shift. And the discipline of Shakespeare studies has been at the epicentre of this shift. Indeed, it has been Shakespeare scholars who have played a major role in several of the theoretical and critical developments (e.g. new historicism, cultural materialism, presentism) that have shaped the discipline of English studies in recent years. Yet a comprehensive scholarly analysis of these crucial developments has yet to be done, and is long overdue. As the first series to foreground analysis of contemporary theoretical developments in the discipline of Shakespeare studies, *Arden Shakespeare and Theory* aims to fill a yawning gap.

To the delight of some and the chagrin of others, since 1980 or so, theory has dominated Shakespeare studies. *Arden Shakespeare and Theory* focuses on the state of the art at the outset of the twenty-first century. For the first time, it provides a comprehensive analysis of the theoretical developments that are emerging at the present moment, as well as those that are dominant or residual in Shakespeare studies.

Each volume in the series aims to offer the reader the following components: to provide a clear definition of a particular theory; to explain its key concepts; to trace its major developments, theorists, and critics; to perform a reading of a Shakespeare text; to elucidate a specific theory's intersection with or relationship to other theories; to situate it in the context of contemporary political, social, and economic developments; to analyse its significance in Shakespeare studies; and to suggest resources for further investigation. Authors of individual volumes thereby attempt to strike a balance, bringing their unique expertise, experience, and perspectives to bear upon particular theories while simultaneously fulfilling the common purpose of the series. Individual volumes in the series are devoted to elucidating particular theoretical perspectives, such as cultural materialism, ecocriticism, ecofeminism, economic theory, feminism, film theory, new historicism, postcoloniality, posthumanism, presentism, psychoanalysis, queer theory, and race theory.

Arden Shakespeare and Theory aims to enable scholars, teachers, and students alike to define their own theoretical strategies and refine their own critical practices. And students have as much at stake in these theoretical and critical enterprises – in the reading and the writing practices that characterize our discipline – as do scholars and teachers. Janus-like, the series looks forward as well as backward, serving as an inspiration and a guide for new work in Shakespeare studies at the outset of the twenty-first century, on the one hand, and providing a retrospective analysis of the intellectual labour that has been accomplished in recent years, on the other.

To return to the beginning: what is at stake in our reading of literary texts? Once we come to understand the various ways in which theory resonates with not only Shakespeare's texts, and literary texts, but the so-called 'real' world – the world outside the world of the mind, the world outside the world of academia – then we come to understand that theory is capable of powerfully enriching not only our reading of Shakespeare's texts, and literary texts, but our lives.

* * *

I am indebted to David Avital, Publisher at Bloomsbury Academic, who was instrumental in developing the idea of the *Arden Shakespeare and Theory* series. I am also grateful to Margaret Bartley, Publisher for Arden Shakespeare, for her guidance and support throughout the development of this series.

Evelyn Gajowski
Series Editor
University of Nevada, Las Vegas

ACKNOWLEDGEMENTS

For their kindness, advice and support in the preparation of this book I should like to thank Siân Adiseshiah, Margaret Bartley, Catherine Belsey, Ruth Charnock, Owen Clayton, Amy Culley, Jonathan Dollimore, John Drakakis, Evelyn Gajowski, Rupert Hildyard, Rebecca Styler, my parents John and Linda, my sister Alison, and most of all my partner Annabelle Mooney. All errors and omissions are, unfortunately, my own.

Introduction

In the last two decades of the twentieth century, Shakespeare's work began to be read in a new, and for many a disconcerting, manner. No longer in thrall to a criticism that dealt with the textual artefact in isolation, a small band of radical literary scholars turned away from the preoccupations of their predecessors and began to pay close attention to the relationship between texts and their contexts. Two distinct approaches developed: new historicism and cultural materialism. Scholars of both persuasions assert that no work can be properly understood unless it is considered alongside the culture of the era from which it has emerged, but it is cultural materialism that offers the most provocative account of the relationship between the past and the text. To quote Jonathan Dollimore, one of the founders of cultural materialism, it offers 'not so much new readings of Shakespeare's texts as a historical relocation of them, one which radically alters the meanings traditionally ascribed to them'.[1] That radical relocation is orientated according to two further coordinates: an engagement with philosophy – particularly that of a Marxist inflection – and, most importantly, a political commitment to progressive causes. Thus, at its best, cultural materialist work is surprising, challenging and supremely relevant. It examines power, the connection between the past and the present, the clash between dominant cultural forms and dissident ideas, and asks two questions that students struggle with day after day: what is the relationship between a text and the human culture that has produced it, and what is the point of literary criticism? This book considers cultural materialism's answers to those questions.

There is no single answer to the question 'What is cultural materialism?'. As Dollimore notes, 'cultural materialism was never ... an abstract theory fixed at the moment of its inception. It was a philosophically informed critical practice and, as such, an evolving project.'[2] The title of this book is therefore a misnomer: cultural materialism is not a theory, but rather a way of reading. Nevertheless, it has definite principles and allegiances, and these have perhaps been most efficiently defined in the foreword to the first edition of *Political Shakespeare: Essays in Cultural Materialism* as 'a combination of historical context, theoretical method, political commitment and textual analysis'.[3] Above all else, cultural materialists consider texts from a materialist rather than an idealist perspective. This means rejecting critical clichés such as the idea that Shakespeare's works demonstrate a revelation of something called 'human nature', and instead paying attention to the actual circumstances in which texts are written and read. Thus, where traditional criticism sees Shakespeare's era as one that comfortably maintained a conservative political status quo, cultural materialism finds evidence of dissent and subversion. Being a materialist also means abandoning the idea that literary criticism exists in a privileged scholarly realm 'above' politics and thus offers unbiased readings of Shakespeare and other literary texts. For cultural materialists, all readings are political readings, not least, of course, their own. Alan Sinfield's answer to the question 'What is cultural materialism?' makes this plain:

> Cultural materialists, basically, wanted to resist the co-option of literature for reactionary tendencies. In the context of rampant capitalist exploitation around the globe, racism at home, and extreme hostility towards the claims of feminism, with Ronald Reagan in the White House and Margaret Thatcher in Downing Street, we believed that the political dimensions of our work had to be paramount.[4]

While the occupants of the White House and 10 Downing Street may have changed, the political issues that Sinfield highlights are still with us. And although in the last thirty years some progress has been made, even a cursory glance at a news bulletin today will reveal that there is a great deal of distance left to be travelled. One of the most disarming things about cultural materialism is that it is upfront about its political concerns: it wants to help make a difference, and while it is not naive about the kind of political role that literary criticism can or cannot play, neither is it embarrassed about openly engaging in material struggles in the world. This more radical political approach is reflected in the topics that cultural materialist work tends to focus on – in particular the representation of marginalized gender, sexual, racial, political and religious groups. Cultural materialism is therefore an approach to texts that emphasizes not their superiority over history and context, but the way that they are linked both with the material conditions of the historical past and, crucially, the political and institutional preoccupations of the present.

No twenty-first-century student can properly appreciate the reception of Shakespeare's work in the last thirty years without an understanding of the cultural materialist approach. This is particularly important because cultural materialism has been so central to Shakespeare criticism, specifically British Shakespeare criticism, that much work influenced by its principles does not explicitly announce itself as cultural materialism at all. Some of the practices that were inaugurated by cultural materialism, particularly the examination of the contexts of production and/or reception of a text, have become commonplace; as Sinfield has remarked, 'cultural materialism has lost its novelty'.[5] However, while the aspect of the methodology that attends to context has broadly been absorbed into the mainstream of literary criticism, the most distinctive characteristic of cultural materialism – its political commitment – has often been lost or ignored. This is not particularly surprising: like most people, academics are usually more comfortable talking about office politics than national politics, and in the face of repeated setbacks the will to continue the political struggle can be hard to muster. Moreover, the academy is just as susceptible to fashion as the rest of the world, and a clamour for the latest style has in recent years resulted in attempts at shuffling cultural materialism, and to a certain extent 'theory' itself, off the stage completely. This tendency has been exemplified by a turn from cultural materialism to what Hugh Grady has called 'the new materialism', a brand of scholarship that analyses the meanings associated with historical objects. Grady finds that shift in phraseology disconcerting:

> the apparently innocent terminological change becomes an ideological bait-and-switch operation when the word 'materialism', which began its life as a term designating a varied tradition of left-wing, political theorising, comes to mean something like 'antiquarianism' … with the effect of effacing political criticism on a large scale.[6]

If the political engagement introduced into Shakespeare studies by cultural materialism and other approaches is allowed to disappear from it entirely, and Shakespeare scholars are forever doomed to talk about the kind of quill Shakespeare used rather than the plays he wrote with it, the discipline runs the risk of being considered nothing more than a remnant of the very past upon which new materialists are so fixated. While retaining a fundamental interest in history, cultural materialist work, as Jonathan Gil Harris notes, also looks in another temporal direction: 'cultural materialism, in its wish for social change, is ostensibly future oriented'.[7] If the future is going to be one worth living, we need cultural materialism more than ever. In an era of isolationism, the retrenchment of many progressive positions, and even creeping fascism, the cultural materialist approach allows students and scholars an opportunity to put the study of Shakespeare to good use. It is far too important to abandon now.

* * *

This book offers a detailed overview of the encounter between cultural materialism and Shakespeare. It would be impossible to chart each separate instance of this encounter; instead, I have concentrated on key examples that set out as clearly as possible how the approach works, why it works in the way that it does and what results it produces. In doing so I have paid special attention to the output of Jonathan Dollimore and Alan Sinfield, the two critics who did the most to establish cultural materialism in the field of literary studies, and who have pursued its implications throughout their careers. However, the work of others – including Catherine Belsey, John Drakakis, Terence Hawkes, Graham Holderness, Ania Loomba and Kathleen McLuskie – is also represented here. Much, although by no means all, of this work emanates from a series of collections on Shakespeare, the influence of which still resonates today. These collections are significant because, as Holderness notes:

> Political criticism, like sex, is something you can't do effectively on your own. On this side of the Atlantic the natural form for radical criticism was the critical anthology, the forum for a collaborative but abrasive conjuncture of different voices ... *Political Shakespeare*, *Alternative Shakespeares*, *The Shakespeare Myth*.[8]

Each of these anthologies is remarkably rich; taken together, they represent a formidable body of work. In what follows I have tried to do justice to this work while at the same time placing it within its own intellectual contexts. This book also puts forward its own readings of Shakespeare, its interpretations of theoretical ideas and methodological debates, and it culminates in a final chapter that presents a cultural materialist reading of Shakespeare's *Julius Caesar*.

Offering interpretations of passages from *Julius Caesar* and *Henry IV, Part 1* as starting points, Chapter 1 begins by explaining the appeal of idealist thinking before setting out the alternative approach offered by cultural materialism. It goes on to examine two key types of Shakespeare criticism that cultural materialists were reacting against: the historicism exemplified by E. M. W. Tillyard and the formalism practised by the New Critics. Both types of criticism are now widely discredited and routinely dismissed, but by paying close attention to readings of Shakespeare I show why this is the case and what cultural materialism has to offer in their place. Chapter 2 adopts a similar structure by juxtaposing cultural materialism with a critical practice from which it dissents, in this case new historicism. With particular reference to a debate about material culture and culture-as-text, the chapter shows what cultural materialism and new historicism have in common, and how they differ. It also charts the influence of the work of Raymond Williams on cultural materialism, and uses *King Henry V* to show how Williams's concepts of dominant, residual and emergent culture can be used as interpretive frameworks through which early modern attitudes towards masculinity can be read. The chapter concludes with an account of the so-called 'subversion/containment debate' that has often been used as a way of demarcating the boundary between new historicism and cultural materialism, and considers the ideological position of both early modern theatre and contemporary Shakespeare criticism.

In Chapter 3 I examine the position taken by cultural materialism on the question of human agency in history. Using a recent debate on this issue between Dollimore and the Shakespearean critic Neema Parvini, I assess claims that cultural materialism adopts the philosophy of anti-humanism. With reference to the work of Louis Althusser and Michel Foucault, I show why this point has often been misunderstood, and clarify the cultural materialist position. The chapter also defends cultural materialism against the charge that it is a 'subjective' form of criticism and illustrates its arguments by beginning and concluding with readings of two very different versions of *Hamlet*. With reference to *Henry V*, *Titus*

Andronicus, *The Tempest* and *The Merchant of Venice*, my fourth chapter deals with the way that cultural materialism relates the Shakespearean past to the contemporary present. After considering what is at stake in the modern-day reception of Shakespeare, the chapter sets out the contribution that cultural materialist work has made in three distinct areas of Shakespeare studies: the teaching of Shakespeare, representations of race and nation, and Shakespearean accounts of gender and sexuality. Special reference is made here to the importance of the Literature Teaching Politics network, and to scholarship that can also be categorized as postcolonialist and feminist.

Chapter 5 constitutes a cultural materialist reading of *Julius Caesar*. Paying close attention to Shakespeare's representation of the Roman plebeians, the chapter argues that the play is capable of being read 'against the grain' to give a more positive account of the relationship between the political classes than has usually been offered. With reference to early modern resistance theory and official reactions to political disobedience, I suggest that from one perspective the plebeians represent an opportunity to construct a polity that functions on egalitarian grounds. However, as the play demonstrates, that potential is also open to grave misuse. The chapter goes on to assess the way that *Julius Caesar* has been used to structure and interpret contemporary politics – specifically the 2016 British EU referendum campaign and the US presidential election – and argues that the historical difference introduced by Shakespeare's play allows us to see our own political moment more clearly. Along the way I consider what Donald Trump learnt from *King Lear*, whether the Roman mob has anything in common with zombie re-imaginings of *Romeo and Juliet*, and why George Clooney represents the dream and the nightmare of the contemporary academic.

1

Cultural Materialism vs 'Old' Historicism and Formalism: 'A Positive (K)not'

Misquotation, misrepresentation and mystification

On the popular book recommendation website Goodreads.com, users have listed their favourite quotations from Shakespeare.[1] At the time of writing, a page entitled 'William Shakespeare Quotes (Author of Romeo and Juliet)' ranks 3,896 quotations attributed to Shakespeare according to the resonance they have for users of the site.[2] First place goes, appropriately enough, to a quotation of a quotation. A total of 37,832 readers 'liked' what Touchstone, the fool in Shakespeare's *As You Like It*, introduces as 'a saying: "The fool doth think he is wise, but the wise man knows himself to be a fool"' (5.1.31–2).[3] Not only does this speak well of the humility to be found in the Goodreads online community, but it is perhaps as appropriate an epigraph as any to a book about Shakespeare, theory and the arguments that these two topics have provoked among critics. But the quotation placed ninth in the list is even more intriguing. Over 6,000 site members voted for the following phrase, attributed only to 'William Shakespeare': 'It is not in the stars to hold our destiny but in ourselves.' An internet search reveals the presence of this quotation on numerous motivational posters, often superimposed upon a star field, or alongside Shakespeare's face, or both. It also turns up on social media sites, in further lists of quotations and in articles on anything from astrology to business studies. It seems clear why the phrase should be so popular: it appeals to a liberal humanist, secular, entrepreneurial consciousness that locates the individual human being as the sole origin of meaning and action. The phrase rejects religious faith and casual super-stition, and ignores any concept of social, governmental or economic frameworks in its support of the sort of solipsistic self-reliant humanism encouraged by Western society since at least the Thatcherite–Reaganite neoconservative politics of the 1980s. As if testifying to the encouraging wholesomeness of Shakespeare's work as opposed to the notorious chaotic vision of Jacobean revenge tragedy, it even neatly echoes and reverses John Webster's fatalistic take on the same topic in *The Duchess of Malfi*: 'We are merely the stars' tennis balls, struck and banded / Which way please them' (5.4.53–4).[4] There's just one problem with these words. Shakespeare didn't write them.

What Shakespeare did write was this: 'The fault, dear Brutus, is not in our stars / But in ourselves, that we are under-lings' (1.2.139–40).[5] These words are spoken by Cassius in the second scene of *Julius Caesar*, first performed in 1599. And to give them their due, 7,581 Goodreads members have selected this as one of their favourite Shakespearean quotations, putting it at number five in the top ten, four places higher than the misquoted version of the same lines.[6] At first sight, perhaps, the general gist of the quotation is not much altered in this accurate version: the idea is still that an individual's fate is in his or her own hands. Nevertheless, a more complex account of human agency is beginning to develop. One way we can see this is to look at the word 'underlings', which offers a much more specific explanation for the 'fault' than is available in the misquoted version. According to the *OED*, 'underling' means 'one who is subject or subordinate to another' and the word was first used (in Middle English) around 1175. 'Underlings' is therefore a political term; it is a way of marking the fact that Brutus and Cassius are, in the society and the time in which they find themselves, less powerful than someone to whom they owe allegiance. Or rather, in Cassius's version of their position, they merely see themselves as less powerful underlings, and it is that misperception that constitutes their fault. Cassius goes on to argue that the real political situation is quite different, and encourages Brutus to stop thinking of himself as a subordinate and begin thinking of himself as a leader. Thus the concept of human agency present in this quotation has moved from the easy cliché of the greetings card to something a little more likely to appear on a protest placard. It's not quite 'Workers of the world, unite. You have nothing to lose but your chains!', but it's not too far off.[7] And the force of that movement from apolitical platitude to revolutionary slogan can be felt even more strongly when it becomes clear that, actually, Shakespeare didn't exactly write these words after all. He misquoted them.

The original source of the lines is the *Confessio Amantis*, or 'The Lover's Confession', a long Middle English poem written in 1390 by John Gower and commissioned by Richard II. Shakespeare certainly knew Gower's work, since a character called John Gower, clearly supposed to be the poet himself, acts as the Presenter in Shakespeare's late Romance *Pericles* and speaks in the verse form used in the *Confessio*.[8] The lines as written by Gower are these:

> The sterres ben of sondri kinde
> And worchen manye sondri thinges
> To ous, that ben here underlinges.[9]

This version is much closer to the fatalism of *The Duchess of Malfi*, where there is no such thing as human agency, and events on earth are the working out of a celestial plan that appears incomprehensible and ridiculous to the human beings that enact and suffer it. It is this that Shakespeare rejects in his revision of Gower; the helplessness of the human being in the face of implacable destiny has in *Julius Caesar* been replaced by the possibility of a human agency located in social consciousness: it is only once Brutus recognizes his place in society that he can try to do something about it. By misquoting Gower's words, Shakespeare demystifies experience, presenting a version of human history that is no longer dominated by abstract forces like 'the stars' but instead by material ones like social position and political power.

It is perhaps time to give a lengthier quotation of Cassius's speech. The subject of these lines is Julius Caesar, who it seems will soon become Emperor of Rome:

> Why, man, he doth bestride the narrow world
> Like a colossus, and we petty men
> Walk under his huge legs and peep about
> To find ourselves dishonourable graves.
> Men at some time are masters of their fates.
> The fault, dear Brutus, is not in our stars
> But in ourselves, that we are underlings.
> 'Brutus' and 'Caesar': what should be in that 'Caesar'?
> Why should that name be sounded more than yours?
> Write them together: yours is as fair a name:
> Sound them, it doth become the mouth as well.
>
> (1.2.134–44)

The line that immediately precedes those I have so far been discussing is especially significant for a reading of the speech as a piece of materialist analysis. Shakespeare has already had Cassius reattribute responsibility for earthly events from the stars to human beings themselves, and to locate the agency of those human beings in the recognition of their socio-political position. By adding the observation that people 'at some time', but, by implication, not at all times, are able to have influence over their circumstances, Cassius suggests that there are limits upon human agency. For him, a consciousness of the real conditions of a society and of the individual's place within those conditions is not enough to enact change; rather, the conditions themselves are beyond individual control and may have a significant bearing upon the success or failure of any revolutionary venture. The same idea is expressed more famously by Brutus in the latter stages of the play, where he remarks:

> There is a tide in the affairs of men
> Which, taken at the flood, leads on to fortune:
> Omitted, all the voyage of their life
> Is bound in shallows and in miseries.
>
> (4.3.216–19)

The notion is reminiscent of one of the founding tenets of the cultural materialist approach, a tenet all the more important because it marks out a key position in the approach's understanding of human agency and the circumstances within which that agency is or is not possible. And while Cassius and Brutus are certainly romanticizing it, at base the idea is a Marxist one and, after Marx, a cultural materialist one. It can be summed up in this phrase, 'men and women make their own history but not in conditions of their own choosing', itself, again, a (deliberate) misquotation.[10] Here there is an acknowledgement of human agency, but a concomitant acknowledgement of its limitations. Sometimes, it may be possible for people to create the means for political change, especially, as is the case for Brutus and Cassius, as part of a group; at other times, it may not – both of those possibilities are beyond the total control of the individual. Thus the human being is neither impotent nor prepotent when it comes to history; the process by which history is made is subject to the culture within which it is made and the political positions that are available within that culture.

Yet to suggest that Cassius's speech is a purely subversive one would be to misrepresent it. While his aim may be the assassination of Caesar, Cassius does not plan to overhaul society completely, and the speech strongly suggests that several aspects of dominant Roman culture will stay in place after his revolution. The first hint that Cassius's call to arms is not quite as materialist as it might have appeared comes in the use of the word 'dishonourable'. Here, Cassius seeks to justify the course of action he is proposing by appealing to Brutus's sense of honour, a code of conduct to which 'good' people are supposed to subscribe. What qualifies as honourable behaviour depends on certain characteristics of the person in question, for example his or her gender, class, rank, age, race and marital status; in this case, upper-class Roman men are speaking, and the spectre of a dishonourable grave is invoked as a token of the grandeur with which such men should live and die. But the problem is that honour is just as much of an abstract force as the stars were. In *Henry IV, Part 1*, as the dissolute knight Sir John Falstaff contemplates the imminent battle of Shrewsbury, he realizes that there is no substance to the concept of honour at all: 'What is honour? A word. What is in that word "honour"? Air. A trim reckoning! Who hath it? He that died o' Wednesday' (5.1.133–6).[11] Penetrating through the layers of mystification surrounding the code, Falstaff points out that honour is nothing more than an empty word that might perhaps give authority to the speaker, but will ultimately be of no practical use. It conditions the way that human actions are understood, but it is a principle drawn from the imagination and imposed upon the human world, rather than one based upon how that world actually exists. Both the honour code and a belief in destiny can therefore be understood as forms of idealism, in the sense that they are explanatory narratives told about human behaviour that have no basis in the evidence of that behaviour itself. They refer to what is abstract rather than to what is material.

Cassius is also invoking the discourse of honour when he makes reference to Brutus' name. At first it sounds as though he is considering the name in a materialistic manner by comparing its actual sound and written appearance to another name, 'Caesar'.

Cassius asks whether there is anything in the name 'Brutus' that explains why it is less acclaimed (or 'sounded') than 'Caesar'. But this supposedly materialist linguistic enquiry is merely a ruse: Cassius is well aware that the power of Caesar does not lie in the aural and visual aspects of his name, just as he is aware that those same qualities of Brutus's name will not be able to provoke an uprising. Rather, Cassius is alluding to the associations that those names have for his Roman contemporaries. Julius Caesar was of course the preeminent statesman of his day, and his great political and military successes, including the conquest of Gaul and the defeat of his former ally Pompey in a civil war, ensured his fame not only in his own time but throughout history. Brutus is probably best known to modern readers through Shakespeare's dramatization in this very play, but in the Roman era the case was different. As G. L. Kittredge, editor of the 1936 *Complete Works*, notes in a gloss to these lines, 'the name Caesar, in fact, until Julius had made it famous, was an insignificant name in history, but *Brutus* – why, it was the greatest name in Roman annals'.[12] As the play goes on to clarify, in ancient Rome the name 'Brutus' was associated most powerfully with Lucius Junius Brutus, who was said to have founded the Roman Republic itself after defeating the tyrant Tarquinius Superbus.[13] So, notwithstanding his membership of one of the upper-class patrician families, Julius Caesar was the maker of his own reputation; by contrast, Brutus's reputation was judged against that of his illustrious forebear, and it is this disparity between the acclaim that met past deeds and the potential acclaim with which future deeds might be received that Cassius plays upon when he says:

> There was a Brutus once that would have brooked
> Th'eternal devil to keep his state in Rome
> As easily as a king.

> (1.2.158–60)

Once again, imagined relations are invoked as justifications for action. In this case an ancient political situation, the imperial rule of the Tarquins, is equated to a contemporary one, the imperial rule of Caesar, not through an analysis of the material conditions of those situations, but via an appeal to the good name of an upper-class family. This is no different from an appeal to the stars. Thus the subversive potential of what seemed at first to be a rejection of idealism in favour of an analysis of material conditions is ultimately contained by a fall back into a more conventional account of a politics dominated by mystifying discourses of honour and reputation. And capping all this is the fact that our would-be revolutionaries are themselves what amounts to aristocratic members of Roman society and as such perhaps less interested in preserving the limited democracy of the state than in preserving their own power within it.

At stake in these various quotations and misquotations are some of the central debates of cultural materialism, debates that will be addressed at much greater length in this book. Like Cassius, cultural materialism is interested in the relationship between people and the political circumstances in which they find themselves, but it goes further than him in its rejection of idealist or metaphysical conceptions of that relationship. Similarly, it takes seriously the possibility of the effective subversion of the dominant order while remaining well aware of just how difficult this can be. All too often the potential for political dissidence is undermined or contained by the re-emergence of dominant thinking, as was the case with Cassius and the issues of honour and social class. The question of human agency has been emphasized because the cultural materialist position on this continues to cause controversy and misunderstanding; it was, for example, the subject of a forthright exchange of words between Neema Parvini and Jonathan Dollimore in various scholarly publications from 2012 to 2015.[14] I will show that one of the best ways to understand cultural materialism is to look closely at the debates that have broken out in its wake. Indeed, cultural materialism itself is a product of dissent from the status quo, although it would be fair to say that that status quo has now shifted far nearer to the territory of the cultural materialists than was formerly the case. I think cultural materialists broadly represented their disagreements with their critical forebears in a fair and accurate manner; nevertheless, misquotations, misrepresentations and mistakes can be revealing, and I will offer one more variation on this theme as a way of developing the notion that cultural materialist practices react against the various methodologies that preceded them.

An interesting misprint occurs in Alan Sinfield's introduction to the second part of *Political Shakespeare* that encapsulates rather nicely the attitude that cultural materialism takes to its critical forebears as well as the politics that it adopts. As I will go on to show, this collection, edited by Dollimore and Sinfield, signalled the emergence of cultural materialism as an iconoclastic approach to Shakespeare's work, and acted as a warning to those critics who would seek to align that work with the political status quo. Yet when introducing the chapters that are to follow, Sinfield adopts a cautious tone, and suggests that Shakespeare might always remain bound up with conservative cultural politics and institutions. Nevertheless, he assures the reader that *Political Shakespeare* will take a constructive view of what he calls the possibilities of 'cultural intervention'. Then comes this phrase: 'We conclude on a positive not [*sic*].'[15] The final word is clearly an error for 'note', but the coinage 'positive not' seems a highly appropriate allusion to cultural materialism. The phrase captures the idea of turning away from established critical methods – to be examined in the next two sections of this chapter – but of doing so in a manner full of optimism that a better way of thinking about Shakespeare, and indeed a better world, is possible. Cultural materialism came about not as an arbitrary change of critical fashion nor as the careerist creation of a bandwagon to jump aboard. Much less was it a response to changes in higher education funding policies or other governmental whims. And neither, despite the views of some of its detractors, is cultural materialism nihilistic: it is predicated upon the possibility of positive change. At the same time, it knows what it is against, what it is not for – something that cannot always be said for some types of theory.

As Dollimore notes in the final sentence of his first monograph *Radical Tragedy*, cultural materialist approaches 'vindicate certain objectives: not essence but potential, not the human condition but cultural difference, not destiny but collectively identified goals'.[16] In this sense, that 'not' is also a 'knot', one which binds cultural materialism as textual analysis to cultural materialism as material practice.

Not 'old' historicism

My first experience of teaching Shakespeare occurred in less than ideal circumstances. I had taken over a first-year drama survey module in the middle of the semester and at short notice; Shakespeare had already been covered, and more contemporary plays, Brian Friel's *Translations* and Caryl Churchill's *Cloud 9*, were next on the syllabus. As the weeks went by, the students seemed happy with our discussions of these works and the issues they addressed, even though some of those issues were quite challenging: British cultural imperialism, military atrocity and armed resistance in Friel; racism, sexism and sexual experimentation in Churchill. In the last few sessions, students were required to give presentations on any aspect of the module that had interested them, and one student chose to talk about the long soliloquy given by Katherina in the final scene of *The Taming of the Shrew*. The speech is a well-known crux; in it, Katherina seems to argue that it is right and natural for wives to be ruled by their husbands:

> Thy husband is thy lord, thy life, thy keeper,
> Thy head, thy sovereign: one that cares for thee
> ...
> And craves no other tribute at thy hands
> But love, fair looks and true obedience –
> Too little payment for so great a debt.
>
> (5.2.152–3, 158–60)[17]

The question is whether these words are sincere and therefore an indication that Katherina has capitulated to the sexist culture she has been struggling against throughout the play, or whether they can be heard, perhaps ironically, as a rejection of that very position. After the student had put forward the first reading, I tentatively suggested that perhaps the alternative interpretation might be available. But my student was having none of this. When I asked her why she wasn't willing to reconsider, she replied: 'Because that's just how things were in those days.' Where, I wondered, had she picked up that idea? And why was it that the radical notions prompted by Friel and Churchill were abandoned when it came to Shakespeare?

Short of being able actually to travel backwards in time, three positions are available to those evaluating the relationship between the past and the present: 'things were so much worse then', 'things were so much better then' or 'things were just the same then'. Generations of children and adults have been entertained and educated by the first alternative, which regularly includes juicy stories of what appear to the present age to be the hardships, humiliations and outrages of previous eras. Equally, they have been beguiled by the artistic glories and military triumphs that are the celebratory meat and drink of the second view. The third possibility offers the pleasures of recognition and the bland reassurance that there is nothing new under the sun. None of these positions is inherently wrong. A great deal depends upon precisely who things may or may not have been better or different for, and exactly when such experiences occurred. The issue, in other words, is to pay attention to nuances and to avoid generalizations. These kinds of fine discriminations are very difficult to make, but other difficulties arise when they fail to occur or are rejected out of hand. No doubt my student had read or had been told at some earlier point in her studies that in Shakespeare's era the lives of women were dominated by men and she had applied that piece of historical background to her reading of *The Taming of the Shrew*.[18] It is of course perfectly true that early modern women very often did find themselves being treated as inferior members of Elizabethan and Jacobean society.[19] But the crucial point is that it does not necessarily follow that it was therefore impossible for women or men, first, to recognize such treatment as unfair and, second, to do something about it. To argue that, whether for better or worse, 'that's just how things were' is to posit an unvarying past in which the voice of authority – the authority that encouraged women to submit to the will of their father or husband, for example – is the only voice that can be heard. And the notion that things were just the same in the past as they are now is even more damaging because it suggests that the values of the present moment are correct and eternal. In fact, such values usually amount to little more than the voice of authority in the present misrecognizing its counterpart in the past. As Dollimore points out, 'the enduring truths which idealist critics found in literature have all too often turned out to be the conservative social and political values one would expect someone of their time and class to hold'.[20] Such an approach is tantamount to the critic's rejection of their responsibility to sift and evaluate the events of the past and the effect of writing, literary or not, on and in history. On the grounds of race, class, gender, sexuality, nationality and religious belief, cultural materialists put long held critical assumptions about the past under a great deal of pressure, and at the very least have increased the visibility of progressive issues in academic discourse and in the academy itself. In this section I examine one of the key places that traditional critical attitudes could be found and show why they were mistaken. If I could actually travel back in time to that drama seminar, this is what I would tell my student.

The name E. M. W. Tillyard is enough to strike horror into the hearts of cultural materialists everywhere. For more than forty years, his work has been held up as the epitome of all that was wrong with the way that history had been brought to bear on readings of Shakespeare and as one of the primary sources of the 'that's just how things were' argument. As early as 1985, Dollimore and Sinfield were calling critical objections to Tillyard's work 'familiar enough'.[21] Despite this, it is essential to examine Tillyard and his views in order to form a proper impression of what exactly cultural materialism was reacting against at its inception. The back-cover blurb of the 1968 reprint of Tillyard's *The Elizabethan World Picture*, first published in 1943, is a good place to start. In it, we learn the following:

> In this short study Dr Tillyard not only elucidates such fairly familiar – though often mystifying – concepts as the four elements, the celestial harmony of 'the nine enfolded Sphears', or macrocosm and microcosm: he also shows how this world picture was variously regarded as a chain of being, a network of correspondences, and a cosmic dance.[22]

'Mystifying' is a wonderful word to choose. The writer of the blurb probably used it to mean 'confusing' and to make a pair with 'familiar', as if to reassure readers who had heard of the four elements, and perhaps even the 'nine enfolded sphears', that they couldn't be blamed for not having understood them properly. But these concepts are also 'mystifying' in a broadly Marxist sense. For Marx, mystification is at the heart of what he calls 'capital', which is defined as 'a *social relation between men* which appears as a relation between things or between men and things'.[23] As this suggests, capital obscures the real relations between people so that the collective work that they do – what Marx calls '*socialized labour*' – is understood by the economy abstractly as 'the *productive power of capital*'. In other words, the human beings who have produced something by their shared labour are overlooked so that social relations are understood instead as economic relations that seem to be completely divorced from actual people and actual work. Marx calls this 'the mystification implicit in the relations of capital as a whole'.[24] In a similar way, Tillyard's project in *The Elizabethan World Picture* was to overwrite the various real actions, relations and ideas of Elizabethan people with mystificatory versions of them that tended to be in the service of state and religious authority. As Dollimore puts it, 'the error, from a materialist perspective, is falsely to unify history and social process in the name of "the collective mind of the people"'.[25] Tillyard's four elements and the like, therefore, are mystifying not because of their complexity, but because of their complicity.

The advertised composition of Tillyard's world picture – 'as a chain of being, a network of correspondences, and a cosmic dance' – holds out the possibility of at least some play in the ordered system that is being proposed. For, while a chain suggests a rigid taxonomy, a network sounds much looser and a dance looser still. If the reader harbours any hopes in this direction he or she will be disappointed by a glance at the book's contents page, which offers sixty-six pages on the chain, with just nineteen on the network and a mere six on the dance. This organization turns out to be an accurate reflection of Tillyard's argument, the tone of which is set early on with reference to the following speech by Ulysses from Shakespeare's *Troilus and Cressida*:

> The heavens themselves, the planets and this centre
> Observe degree, priority and place,
> Insisture, course, proportion, season, form,
> Office and custom, in all line of order.
> ...
> O, when degree is shaked,
> Which is the ladder to all high designs,
> The enterprise is sick. How could communities,
> Degrees in schools and brotherhoods in cities,
> Peaceful commerce from dividable shores,
> The primogeneity and due of birth,
> Prerogative of age, crowns, sceptres, laurels,
> But by degree stand in authentic place?
> Take but degree away, untune that string,
> And hark what discord follows.
>
> (1.3.85–8, 101–10)[26]

Tillyard remarks, 'much of what I have to expound is contained in this passage' and, true to his word, he returns to it repeatedly, each time emphasizing the fundamental place it occupies in his idea of universal order and, significantly, leaning upon the authority of Shakespeare when doing so.[27] For example, Tillyard's chain of being, which ranked the importance of every part of creation and 'stretched from the foot of God's throne to the meanest of inanimate objects',[28] is 'a traditional way of describing the world-order hinted at by Shakespeare in Ulysses' speech'.[29] Tillyard's 'network' version of the world picture is described as 'a number of planes, arranged one below another in order of dignity but connected by an immense net of correspondences'.[30] Once again, Shakespeare is invoked to guarantee the validity of this view: 'one reason why Ulysses' speech on "degree" in *Troilus and Cressida* is so rich is that here Shakespeare uses the great correspondences in all possible ways'.[31] Even the cosmic dance, which 'implies "degree", but degree in motion', is endorsed with the final two lines of Ulysses' speech quoted above, which Tillyard claims shows Shakespeare's 'knowledge of the general doctrine'.[32] This is all made even more explicit in Tillyard's next book, *Shakespeare's History Plays*, where he takes for granted that 'most readers of Shakespeare know that his own version of order or degree is Ulysses' speech on the topic in *Troilus and Cressida*'.[33]

The first problem with Tillyard's thesis is his use of this speech. In common with many critics of his generation and earlier, Tillyard takes Ulysses' words for Shakespeare's, ignoring the circumstances within which they are spoken and the fact that the views of a character may not necessarily align with those of its author.[34] In some cases the consequences of such critical tone-deafness can be trivial, but since Tillyard undoubtedly chose to foreground Shakespeare's work precisely because of its cultural significance, the claim that Shakespeare believed what he had Ulysses say is a serious one. Margot Heinemann offers an excellent example of just how serious this can get in her essay for *Political Shakespeare*. Heinemann quotes from a 1983 newspaper interview with Nigel Lawson, then British Chancellor of the Exchequer, who refers to Ulysses' speech in order to defend his own critique of egalitarianism. The Chancellor says of the speech, 'the fact of differences, and the need for some kind of hierarchy, both these facts, are expressed more powerfully there than anywhere else I know in literature ... Shakespeare was a Tory, without any doubt.'[35] Lawson makes explicit what was implicit in Tillyard: here, Shakespeare is used in an overtly ideological manner by one of the most powerful politicians in the land to justify a course of action that his government was taking – to the detriment of millions of people, it should be added. In that it promoted a static version of human relations backed by ideology, Tillyard's use of the speech in *The Elizabethan World Picture* was itself political, although it is unlikely Tillyard would have seen it that way. In turn Lawson makes the speech party political and, as Heinemann notes, in doing so makes us 'see more clearly what the struggle over the meanings of Shakespeare is really about'.[36] Her point, a classic cultural materialist insight, is that whoever claims that Shakespeare is speaking on their behalf adds a huge amount of cultural authority to what they have to say. Of course, absent from Lawson's account of the speech, just as it is from Tillyard's, is the context within which it is spoken. Heinemann notes that 'Ulysses may talk about the sacredness of hierarchy and order, but the setting shows him as a cunning politician whose behaviour undercuts what he says here, as indeed does the whole play'.[37] Moreover, as Catherine Belsey points out, 'thanks to his part in smuggling the wooden horse into Troy, Ulysses was a byword for untrustworthiness in early modern England'.[38] Rather than justifying the principle of order and degree, on this basis it would be more reasonable to argue that *Troilus and Cressida* exposes the bankruptcy of a political elite that not only uses such ideas to naturalize its own power but also ignores them when they prove inconvenient.

Nevertheless, it would be wrong to suggest that Tillyard's schema is without merit. Many Elizabethans certainly did conceive of the workings of the universe in the ways that he sets out; moreover, there are moments at which Tillyard concedes that dissent from such opinions was possible. However, the problem is that despite this the book gives the strong impression that such beliefs were shared by all; for John Drakakis, 'at best it sustained an ideology, an illusion and, by definition, a distortion of "reality"'.[39] For example, and to return to the topic with which this chapter began, in a section subtitled 'The stars and fortune' Tillyard offers the following sentence: 'whether he were scrupulously orthodox or inclined to instinctive superstition, the Elizabethan believed in the pervasive operation of an external fate in the world'.[40] As I have already shown, Cassius has a different idea. Despite this confident assertion, a few sentences later Tillyard softens his judgement a little to suggest that there were indeed those who were sceptical about the influence of the stars, but in his view 'the general trend was of belief'.[41] In fact, this is not the only point at which a glimmer of such resistance can be perceived. As Gabriel Egan points out,

> Tillyard did not leave human agency, especially subversion, out of his model, as is often claimed: it is there, for example, in the stars being supposed intermediaries between Fortune and human affairs, obeying God's changeless order yet responsible for the vagaries of luck in the sublunar realm.[42]

Egan highlights Tillyard's own proviso that the 'doctrine that our wills are our own and that the stars' influence can be resisted may not be sufficiently recognized, the typical Elizabethan habit of mind being too often taken to be one of desperate recognition of an ineluctable fate'.[43] But notwithstanding such caveats, the real issue is that Tillyard himself has not sufficiently recognized the potential for resistance he mentions here, and, as in the above quotation, too often dismisses it by falling back into general claims about what 'the Elizabethan believed'.

To illustrate this further, it is worth noticing which Shakespearean characters are thought by Tillyard to be able to see through the prevailing ideology. Edmund from *King*

Lear gets significant attention, not unexpectedly given that character's well-known scepticism of cosmic influences on human affairs. In response to his father's claim that troubling events in the kingdom have been caused by recent solar and lunar eclipses, Edmund remarks in a soliloquy: 'This is the excellent foppery of the world, that when we are sick in fortune, often the surfeits of our own behaviour, we make guilty of our disasters the sun, the moon and the stars' (1.2.118–21).[44] For Tillyard, the speech confirms Edmund's villainy, but he also sees Edmund as 'justly the critic of his father's superstitions'. None the less, the potential for human agency that thus becomes available here is quickly cast into doubt when Tillyard suggests that 'we may be meant to look on Edmund as one of those superlatively vicious men whom the stars and their wills have joined to produce'.[45] Here human agency collapses into supernatural destiny, since an agency that comes to pass only according to the will of the heavens is no agency at all. Moreover, the force of that unevidenced 'we may be meant' once again emphasizes a reactionary view of the matter, where even those who rail against the absurdity of astrology are unavoidably captured by it. By contrast, in *The Tempest* Prospero is thought by Tillyard to be able to defy and even control the stars, while Caliban is 'too much under the sky's dominance ever to be other than he is'.[46] Such judgements will come as no surprise to postcolonial critics of Shakespeare, who have long noted the way that Prospero has been seen by some interpreters as a shining ideal of European civilization while Caliban is the abhorrent other too primitive to benefit from the care of his benevolent master.[47] The impression given is that only those characters of whom Tillyard approves are granted the virtue of human agency, while the rest are abandoned to their fates. For them, that's just the way things were.

If cultural materialist objections to Tillyard were located purely upon ideological grounds they might be of only limited interest to readers and critics of Shakespeare. But the fundamental point in all of this is that Tillyard's privileging of order and degree leaves him with little to say about Shakespeare's work when such order is challenged; by contrast, cultural materialist readings thrive upon such challenges. Competing analyses of *King Henry V* offer a useful example of this difference. In *Shakespeare's History Plays*, Tillyard remarks that *Henry V* 'shows a great falling off in quality' when compared to those plays that precede it in the second tetralogy.[48] He seems baffled by the play, and the elements that Tillyard finds most troublesome are, unsurprisingly, those that fail to integrate with his overarching theme. The high treason of the Earl of Cambridge, Lord Scrope and Sir Thomas Grey, revealed by Henry in 2.2, gives Tillyard a great deal of difficulty. He calls Henry's reproof to Scrope 'alien in tone to the norm of the play' and suggests that such treachery, understood as 'the unbelievable contradiction of appearance and reality',

> has nothing to do with the matters that have most been the concern of this book: with politics, with patterns of history, with ancestral curses, with England's destiny and all the order of her society. It is a personal and not a public theme.[49]

In a play that takes pains to show how a range of characters across many levels of British and Irish society react to war, the notion that the treachery of some at the very pinnacle of that society is not 'a public theme' seems shortsighted to say the least. But that is the kind of conclusion arrived at by critics who cannot accept that Shakespeare's plays might wish to interrogate the idea that a successful society is based on principles of order and degree. Tillyard can only explain Henry's speech denouncing Scrope by supposing that Shakespeare 'is drawing on personal experience and filling up the gap with an account of how someone at some time let him, Shakespeare, down'.[50] This is pretty desperate stuff. Similarly, Henry's well-known soliloquy on the burden of kingship, itself prompted by his clandestine encounter with soldiers who probe the disguised king's authority, is called by Tillyard 'somehow extrinsic to the play, a piece of detached eloquence'.[51] He cannot see that *Henry V* is not interested in simply reinforcing set ideas about authority, but in investigating the challenges authority faces and the strategies it uses to sustain itself.

By contrast, these two dramatic incidents offer a key for Dollimore and Sinfield's cultural materialist reading of *Henry V*. Both the treason of the noblemen and Henry's meditation on kingship reveal what they call the play's 'obsessive preoccupation' with insurrection.[52] Henry's execution of the elite traitors and his ultimate assuagement of the doubts of common soldiers through victory at Agincourt might at first appear to be a dismissal of the forces of insurrection; as Dollimore and Sinfield note, 'the play seems, in one aspect, committed to the aesthetic colonization of such elements in Elizabethan culture'.[53] In other words, if the forces of insurrection in the play are not going to be ignored outright as they are by Tillyard, one way of dealing with them might be to acknowledge their presence in the play but show how effectively they are neutralized by its end. In this sense the play could be said to 'colonize' those forces: it dramatizes potential rebellion specifically in order to dramatize the frustration of that rebellion. However, such a reading cannot be said to take us very far away from Tillyard. Indeed, while he was dissatisfied with the play because the importance of order and degree was displaced within it, a reading that identifies that order *in extremis* but then demonstrates how it revitalizes itself remains entirely upon Tillyard's terrain. A further step is necessary. In fact, Dollimore and Sinfield acknowledge that in their view the play does not support what might be called a neo-Tillyardian interpretation. Rather, they show that something much more provocative is occurring. The play certainly reveals the existence of threats to the hierarchical order that pervades its world, but Dollimore and Sinfield do not accept that the play closes these down. Instead they argue that

Henry V can be read to reveal not only the rulers' strategies of power, but also the anxieties informing both them and their ideological representation. In the Elizabethan theatre to foreground and even to promote such representations was not to foreclose on their interrogation.[54]

Nowhere is the anxiety that informs the master theme of order shown more clearly than in these lines that form part of the king's speech dismissed by Tillyard as 'detached eloquence':

O ceremony, show me but thy worth!
What is thy soul of adoration?
Art thou aught else but place, degree, and form,
Creating awe and fear in other men?
Wherein thou art less happy, being fear'd,
Than they in fearing.

$(4.1.241-6)$[55]

It is perhaps not surprising that Tillyard came unstuck at this point, where the principle he had championed so faithfully is demystified by the figure of the monarch himself. Here Henry calls the nature of his power into question by drawing attention to the ideological basis of the hierarchical structure from which it emanates, while at the same time lamenting his dominant position within it. By inviting us to pity him, for Drakakis Henry 'manipulates those symbols from which he seeks some temporary disengagement in order to elicit sympathy for what we might call, with the benefit of hindsight, "the management interest"'.[56] The strategy is a canny one, since if that audience sympathy is given and the king is thus thought to be the real victim of order and degree, the system that Henry here bemoans is left more secure than ever. None the less, Dollimore and Sinfield's point is not simply that through the play 'the ideological dimension of authority ... [is] rendered vulnerable to demystification'.[57] For, in drawing attention to the flaws and anxieties of the monarchical ideology present in the play, they also disclose how cultural materialist criticism engages with Elizabethan history in a new way.

Responding once more to the speech on ceremony, Dollimore and Sinfield note that 'how far the king's argument is to be credited is a standard question for conventional criticism, but a materialist analysis takes several steps back and reads real historical conflict in and through his ambiguities'.[58] Here we can see clearly how for cultural materialists texts are connected, or 'knotted', to the material circumstances in which they were produced and received. Instead of labelling the king's speech with the politically quietist mark of ambiguity, Dollimore and Sinfield look for what might be the causes of the impasse Henry finds himself in. For *Henry V*, those real historical conflicts include English colonial adventures in Ireland, a connection the play makes explicit with a reference to a contemporaneous Irish military campaign led by the Earl of Essex; troubled relations between neighbouring nations of the British Isles, addressed through the appearance of army captains from England, Ireland, Scotland and Wales; the potential lower-class disaffection of the soldiers Henry visits in disguise as well as his old companions Bardolph, Pistol and Nym; and the high treason of the nobility. Henry's speech, then, while 'eloquent', is anything but 'detached'. On the contrary, Dollimore and Sinfield see its attachment to Elizabethan culture as fundamental to its effect: the speech and the play as a whole are attempts to work through some of the very real concerns of Shakespeare's culture. In the course of this working through, some resolutions are proposed; for example, Henry's triumph at Agincourt can easily be read as an imagined version of Essex's hoped-for triumph in Ireland. It is understandable that the play should offer 'a displaced, imaginary resolution' to at least some of these problems – fantasy is, after all, often the only avenue open to those who have no real power to end their troubles.[59] But while some problems are fantastically resolved, others are exposed by those very resolutions. Thus the fantasy figure of an ideal monarch like Henry V – the sole source of all meaning and authority in his society – is, as we have seen, constantly threatened by insurrection as well as the burdens of that position itself.

Human affairs are not ruled by astrology or ordered by a self-perpetuating chain of being. These are simply narratives superimposed upon the real relationships and events that occur in the world in an attempt to assert authority over them. Critics like Tillyard tended to suggest that such narratives, while complex, were stable and assented to by all. Cultural materialists agree that the relationship between events and meanings is complex, but insist upon the instability of authoritative ideologies and their availability for subversion. The resigned sense that 'that's just how things were in those days' is not one that is accepted by cultural materialist critics.

Not formalism

If Tillyard's interpretive practice was compromised by the erroneous assumption that a fixed cosmic order was accepted by Shakespeare and the majority of early modern citizens, formalist critics looked for a sense of unity not in the contexts of the text but in the text itself, paying little or no attention to the conditions within which it was written and would be read. As Raymond Williams puts it, formalism's 'predominant emphasis was on the specific, intrinsic characteristics of a literary work, which required analysis "in its own terms" before any other kind of discussion, and especially social or ideological analysis, was relevant or even possible'.[60] Some of the most influential critical methodologies of the twentieth century were, to some extent or another, formalist in sympathy, from the Russian Formalists in the 1920s, the Practical Critics and American New Critics during the middle of the century, to some versions of poststructuralism in more recent decades. While their approaches vary, each of these schools treat the literary text as a self-enclosed phenomenon located within a realm far removed from the mundane one in which, for example, early modern playwrights worry about getting their plays approved by the Master of the Revels, and early modern playgoers wonder which inn to patronize after the play has finished. Such concerns were not considered the province of literary studies, a branch of knowledge often defined by its very opposition to the everyday material conditions in which, among other things, texts are produced and experienced. Formalism, then, in its opposition to these material concerns, is a kind of idealism. Nevertheless, it would be irresponsible to ignore the successful insights that formalist modes of criticism have produced. The Russian Formalists, for example, reinvented what could be done in literary studies through their close attention to the subtleties of narrative, while the New Critics produced many elegant and persuasive close readings of complex texts. And in Shakespeare studies, it is important to understand what leading formalist critics L. C. Knights and G. Wilson Knight, who had no interest in historicizing the texts they analysed, were themselves reacting against. They turned their attention to 'the words on the page' in an attempt to rid the discipline of the influence of A. C. Bradley, the great critic of plot and character. Indulging too often in a pursuit still common today, Bradley tended to treat Shakespearean characters as if they were real people, and was waspishly mocked for doing so in the title of Knights's famous essay 'How Many Children Had Lady Macbeth?' While there was certainly more to Bradley than asking unanswerable questions, the movement towards a formalist criticism that was not anchored exclusively in the identity and experiences of the Shakespearean character as pseudo-human being was initially a breath of fresh air.

None the less, as Drakakis points out, 'the retreat into formalism, though ostensibly a response to textual anomaly and a desire to analyse internal structure, may also sometimes be seen as a rejection of unfamiliar or unpalatable forms of social analysis'.[61] Such retreats are certainly appealing on a personal level – who hasn't tried to escape from life by turning to a good book, film or record? – but hardly a reasonable position for a discipline of criticism to take. Drakakis's use of the word 'unpalatable' touches upon a deeply outdated but not yet entirely extinguished donnish reluctance to engage with the politics and culture of the present that, even today, lurks in university corridors. Although the humanities must certainly reject purely instrumentalist justifications of their value, a thoroughgoing formalism plays into the hands of those who would characterize the academy's reluctance to engage with politics as 'Ivory Towerism'. Terry Eagleton locates the origin of such reluctance in the decline of a literary 'public sphere' that arose in the seventeenth century and that he defines as 'social institutions – clubs, journals, coffee houses, periodicals – in which private individuals assemble for the free, equal interchange of reasonable discourse, thus welding themselves into a relatively cohesive body whose deliberations may assume the form of a powerful political force'.[62] The rise of the modern capitalist state and the professionalization of the subject of English via the academy contributed to the virtual disappearance of this public sphere by the beginning of the twentieth century, and it is in this situation that formalist modes of criticism began to take precedence over more publicly engaged types of analysis. As Eagleton sees it,

> once the 'public' has become the 'masses', subject to the manipulations of a commercialized culture, and 'public opinion' has degenerated into 'public relations', the classical public sphere must disintegrate, leaving in its wake a deracinated cultural intelligentsia whose plea for 'disinterestedness' is a dismissal of the public rather than an act of solidarity with them.[63]

The picture is of a removed, resentful critical elite that abandoned the social realm of lived experience for something approaching Plato's world of ideal forms.[64]

In the case of New Criticism, idealism is encapsulated in that approach's search for 'unity', itself an almost metaphysical term that refers to the infinitely valuable and perfectly balanced harmony of a great work of literature. In the words of Cleanth Brooks, one of the leading New Critics, 'the primary concern of criticism is with the problem of unity – the kind of whole which the literary work forms or fails to form, and the relation of the various parts to each other in building up this whole'.[65] As Brooks suggests, only certain works achieved this unity, and those that did were treated almost as holy artefacts of a past that remained deliberately uninvestigated. It would not be unfair to see in this prizing of aesthetic unity an echo of the celebration of order that was present in Tillyard's work, and the effect is the same. As Tillyard's rejection of *Henry V* shows, texts that were ideologically or thematically challenging could be dismissed as lacking unity, or, as Sinfield points out, the critic might 'help the text into coherence', something he sees as 'the virtual raison d'être of traditional criticism'.[66] When formalists turn their attention to the text's 'themes', these are 'typically reduced to aspects of the "human condition" – the thematic expression of formalism', with all the traditionalist qualities that that phrase connotes.[67] In the more damning words of Eagleton, reading in the New Critical way

> drove you less to oppose McCarthyism or further civil rights than to experience such pressures as merely partial, no doubt harmoniously balanced somewhere else in the world by their complementary opposites. It was, in other words, a recipe for political inertia, and thus for submission to the political status quo.[68]

An alternative approach is expressed by Pierre Macherey, who notes that '*the postulated unity of the work which, more or less explicitly, has always haunted the enterprise of criticism, must now be denounced*: the work is not *created* by an intention (objective or subjective): it is *produced* under determinate conditions'.[69] It is the analysis of the determinate conditions of reception and production of a text, its face set squarely against political inertia, that characterizes the cultural materialist method.

One final return to *Julius Caesar* is needed to illustrate the difference between the kind of work produced by idealist formalists and that produced by cultural materialists. In his highly influential book *The Wheel of Fire*, G. Wilson Knight reads Shakespeare's works against the Bradleian tradition of character analysis, offering instead a 'poetic interpretation' that pays attention to 'form, pattern and symmetry'.[70] As such he produces engaging close readings of Shakespeare's plays, including a chapter on *Julius Caesar* that juxtaposes what Wilson Knight calls the 'Brutus-theme' with the '*Macbeth* vision'.[71] A reluctance to frame the analysis according to character alone is already clear from that terminology; instead, Brutus and Macbeth are understood more as fields of poetic imagery that dominate certain aspects of their particular plays. None the less, character is still one organizing principle of Wilson Knight's analysis, as his comment on the downfall of the two protagonists demonstrates: 'Both Brutus and Macbeth fail in their schemes not so much because of outward events and forces, but through the working of that part of their natures which originally forbade murder.'[72] Such an argument charts a return to the dialectic of human agency and destiny, but this time that debate has turned within. In Wilson Knight's version, the effects of fate or history are no longer the problem; instead, it is what he calls 'conscience, or instinct, or whatever it was which urged him not to assassinate Caesar' that prevents Brutus from killing Antony and thus securing the insurrection.[73] A cultural materialist intervention would here point out that it makes little difference whether human actions are seen to be frustrated by the stars or some mysterious interior force: each of these concepts is ideological. Like honour and like the stars, 'conscience, or instinct, or whatever' are abstract codes of behaviour that in Wilson Knight's account have been reified into concrete entities. What he seems to be grasping at here is a framework for interpreting the relationship between individual behaviour and social norms that (usually) prevent acts such as murder. Unavailable to Wilson Knight, but a key part of the landscape of literary theory for the last forty-five years, the work of theorists such as Louis Althusser and Michel Foucault offers cultural materialists such a framework. I will discuss Althusser and Foucault at greater length in Chapter 3; however, for now, I'd like, briefly, to show how such theory can signal a way out of Wilson Knight's dead end.

Foucault is helpful to cultural materialists because he offers a method of escaping from one of the most pervasive assumptions of literary criticism: transcendental humanism. According to this concept, the human subject is understood as an unchangeable essence that persists, sometimes shaken but never stirred, throughout brutal local events and the course of history itself. For Foucault, this is simply mystification. Instead, he argues:

> One has to dispense with the constituent subject, to get rid of the subject itself, that's to say, to arrive at an analysis which can account for the constitution of the subject within a historical framework. And this is what I would call genealogy, that is, a form of history which can account for the constitution of knowledges, discourses, domains of objects etc., without having to make reference to a subject which is either transcendental in relation to the field of events or runs in its empty sameness throughout the course of history.[74]

As Foucault suggests, once the idea of a fixed universal subjectivity is rejected, it becomes possible to see human thought and action as contingent upon the knowledges and discourses that are in circulation at any given moment of history. A clear line can be drawn here from Marx's credo that 'men and women make their own history but not in conditions of their own choosing' to the cultural materialist approach: the analysis of texts becomes material in the sense that actual political affiliations and historical events, rather than fuzzy trans-historical notions like 'conscience', can be read on to the plays. This is not, of course, to say that the concept of 'conscience' went unrecognized in Roman or Elizabethan times, but merely that how the concept was actually understood differs in each era, and whether it was obeyed depended upon a range of other material factors such as those dramatized in *Julius Caesar*.

Armed with such ideas, it becomes a relatively straightforward task to critique a typical formalist passage like the following:

> The most obvious forms of symbolism in these two plays are (i) storm-symbolism, (ii) blood-imagery, and (iii) animal-symbolism. ... They stand for contest, destruction, and disorder in the outer world and in the reader's mind, mirroring the contest, destruction, and disorder both in the soul of the hero and in that element of the poet's intuitive experience to which the plays concerned give vivid and concrete dramatic form.[75]

Here, Wilson Knight exchanges Tillyard's concern with order for a concern with disorder, and justifies this move on aesthetic grounds by identifying three fields of imagery that testify to a state of disruption. Revealingly, Wilson Knight describes the effects of that disruption on the 'outer world' (presumably the world of the play) and in the mind of the reader – typically, no thought is given to the play being performed – but he locates the source of that disruption and the symbolism it produces in the hero's 'soul' and the playwright's 'intuitive experience'. Suitably wary of idealism and transcendental humanism, the cultural materialist critic can see that the material conditions responsible for the turmoil of *Julius Caesar* – politics, in other words – have been replaced by an investment in a mysterious subjectivity that is communicated directly from author to reader via the medium of poetic language. The effect that this leaves on the reader of Wilson Knight's essay is one of admiration, both for the talent of Shakespeare and for the skill of Wilson Knight himself. Yet, in the words of Sinfield, 'cultural materialists are beset by the question of what it is all for'.[76] What is the value of an admiration that cannot be put to some use?

One answer is provided by Graham Holderness and Marcus Nevitt who, in a reading of *Julius Caesar* that begins with the same preternatural disruption that Wilson Knight notices, point out the way that such things are easily dismissed by the character Cicero:

> Indeed it is a strange-disposed time.
> But men may construe things after their fashion
> Clean from the purpose of the things themselves.
>
> (1.3.33–5)

Holderness and Nevitt concentrate on the word 'construe', showing how as 'both the act of representation and the act of interpretation, the verb is at the heart of the play's political and hermeneutical structures'.[77] In other words, it is not the origin of storm-, blood- and animal-symbolism that is important in the reality of the play, but what such things are made to *symbolize* in a Rome 'where truth is constructed by powerful men' like Mark Antony. As Holderness and Nevitt note, even at the end of the play Cassius has not grasped the fact that the ability to control the meanings of material events will trump reputation and honour every time: 'Cassius commits suicide tenaciously holding on to the belief that "men are ... masters of their fates" but still tragically unaware as to why Caesar should be "grown so great" compared to Brutus.'[78] The essay then sets out to show how Shakespeare and *Julius Caesar* in particular 'have been "construed" by the political Right in Britain', citing the fact that 'modes of cultural materialist analysis are predicated upon a belief in the continuity of connection between the Renaissance text and the world of contemporary politics and upon the necessity of pledging a political commitment within that world'.[79] This continuity and commitment, then, are 'what it is all for'. In the next chapter I will begin to examine this agenda more closely by considering cultural materialism alongside new historicism, an approach with which it has been frequently associated.

2

Text vs Material: Cultural Materialism and New Historicism

Poetics, materialism and textuality

It is the spring of 2016, and portmanteau words are every-where. In the UK, the talk is of Brexit and Bremain; in the US presidential election, voters will be asked to overlook Hillary Clinton's emailgate if they wish to avert a catastrophic Trumpocalypse. While the rise of social media seems to have increased the rate at which such neologisms are coined, portmanteau words have a long history. Of course, Shakespeare used a great many portmanteaux in his work, including words like 'impiteous' (*Hamlet* 4.5.100), a combi-nation of 'impetuous' and 'piteous', 'intrinsicate' (*Antony and Cleopatra* 5.2.303), from 'intricate' and 'intrinsic', and 'glazed' (*Julius Caesar* 1.3.21), joining together 'gazed' and 'glared'.[1] Such terms are sometimes creatures of necessity, born out of a writer's need to find a word that will fit the iambic pentameter line or the Twitter character limit. More often, they are gifts calculated to cause the reader pleasure in the unexpected or humorous conjunction of two familiar words, or at least to allow him or her to avoid the pain of re-reading the same awkward formulation again and again. Yet such coinages can be problematic if they imply an identity between two linked words that, upon closer inspection, overlooks some significant differences. This has occasionally been the fate of cultural materialism and new historicism, two critical practices that have been conflated into one by some critics, often those whose aim is to dismiss both. Thus in a 1988 essay Carol Thomas Neely refers to 'cult-historicists', a coinage that conjures up visions of hooded figures paying homage by candlelight to an effigy of A. J. P. Taylor.[2] Similarly, in 2015 Neema Parvini refers to Alan Sinfield as 'speaking on behalf of cultural historicists'.[3] Edward Pechter fails to do cultural materialism even the courtesy of including it in a portmanteau when he asserts in passing that the term is Dollimore and Sinfield's 'phrase for the new historicism'.[4] The same strategy is adopted by Jeremy Hawthorn in his book on new historicism and cultural materialism, where he confesses he will 'use "New Historicism/New Historicist" as my blanket terms'.[5] In truth cultural materialism and new historicism share a great deal; the inclusion of essays by well-known new historicists Stephen Greenblatt and Leonard Tennenhouse in Jonathan Dollimore and Alan Sinfield's *Political Shakespeare*, the subtitle of which is *Essays in Cultural Materialism*, suggests as much, and has perhaps caused some of the trouble. So while portmanteaux are understandable, they can lead to misunderstandings. Nevertheless, the relationship between cultural materialism and new historicism is perhaps best captured by another portmanteau, recorded by the *OED* as far back as 1953. They are frenemies.

The early 1980s saw the publication of ground-breaking works of Shakespearean scholarship and criticism, including collections such as Dollimore and Sinfield's *Political Shakespeare,* and *Alternative Shakespeares* edited by John Drakakis (both 1985), as well as monographs such as Dollimore's *Radical Tragedy: Religion, Ideology and Power in the Drama of Shakespeare and his Contemporaries* (1984), and, earliest of all, Stephen Greenblatt's *Renaissance*

Self-Fashioning: From More to Shakespeare (1980). It was no coincidence that these books shared an interest in repudiating the critical orthodoxies I discussed in the previous chapter. By the late 1970s the work of continental thinkers such as Pierre Macherey, Roland Barthes, Antonio Gramsci, Julia Kristeva, Louis Althusser, Jacques Derrida, Michel Foucault and others had been translated into English and disseminated widely, and thus began to find its way into debates about writing and history. As Drakakis puts it, 'forms of revisionary Marxism, feminism, poststructuralism and psychoanalysis all came together in a series of productive tensions'.[6] In their foreword to *Political Shakespeare*, Dollimore and Sinfield remark that these tensions 'brought a new rigour and excitement to literary discussions', and, for them, this energy was channelled into a cultural materialism that exchanged traditionalist, formalist and idealist modes of criticism for politicized historicist analyses grounded in a socialist consciousness.[7] But of course other methodologies were produced by this literary critical 'big bang'. Chief among them, certainly for Shakespeare studies, was new historicism, an approach that was inaugurated by Greenblatt's *Renaissance Self-Fashioning*. While this is not the place to discuss new historicism in depth, in this chapter I will trace the similarities and the differences between it and cultural materialism, paying attention to their shared origins as well as their disagreements.

Greenblatt is disarmingly self-deprecating about the coining of the term new historicism. Writing in 1990, he suggests that its first appearance in his introduction to the edited collection *The Power of Forms in the English Renaissance* was almost accidental: 'out of a kind of desperation to get the introduction done, I wrote that the essays represented something I called a "new historicism" … The name stuck much more than other names I'd very carefully tried to invent over the years.'[8] One of those other names, and perhaps one that more clearly encapsulates exactly what it is that Greenblatt and others are trying to do in their work, is 'cultural poetics'. As described in the opening pages of *Renaissance Self-Fashioning*, cultural poetics is 'a more cultural or anthropological criticism' that understands that both the critic himself or herself and the artefact he or she is analysing are implicated within a cultural structure from which they can never fully escape. For Greenblatt, then,

> a literary criticism that has affinities to this practice must be conscious of its own status as interpretation and intent upon understanding literature as a part of the system of signs that constitutes a given culture; its proper goal, however difficult to realize, is a *poetics of culture*.[9]

It is thus already clear that new historicism shares cultural materialism's conviction that a text cannot be properly understood if it is thought to be divorced from its contexts of production, and no matter how much they strive for objectivity, neither can the critic claim to be divorced from the culture within which they receive it. As I discussed in Chapter 1, once such assumptions are granted they immediately rule out, first, a Tillyardian historicism that fails to account for either its own ideological biases or the competing ideas of the culture within which its object of analysis was created, and, second, a formalism that brackets off the aesthetic from the social.

In attempting the difficult task of cultural poetics, Greenblatt enlists the aid of two allied techniques that are shared with cultural materialist work: he pays attention to non-literary texts and uses historical and contemporary anecdotes to gain some purchase on complex topics. These techniques are allied in the sense that they both invest significance in sources that were previously marginalized in historical and literary studies. The same attitude, this time located in the present, is manifest in Dollimore and Sinfield's comment that in cultural materialism, '"high culture" is taken as one set of signifying practices among others'.[10] But what exactly is the value for criticism of treating such (written and spoken) texts with the same level of analysis that critics previously reserved for canonical works such as Shakespeare's plays? For new historicism, one answer is that such texts can shed light upon the ideas, fears or fantasies that exist in a culture and that perhaps have not previously been detected in literature, or only detected in isolation. Once identified, such discoveries can then be read back into the literary work as a way of unlocking hitherto neglected meanings. A classic example of this occurs in Louis Adrian Montrose's new historicist essay on *A Midsummer Night's Dream*.[11] Montrose begins the piece by quoting from the 1597 diary of an Elizabethan gentleman called Simon Forman. In his diary Forman wrote an account of an erotic dream he had had about Queen Elizabeth I, and Montrose uses this to make a point about the way that the power of Elizabeth as a specifically female monarch resonated throughout the culture for which she served as figurehead. With reference to Titania, Hippolyta and the gender politics of *Dream*, Montrose goes on to consider how Elizabethan culture dealt with ideas about powerful women across a range of cultural texts. But beyond the utility it had for offering a renewed interest in the canon (a factor that is recognized by new historicists as not unproblematic) for Catherine Gallagher and Stephen Greenblatt there is also something powerful in the anecdote on its own terms: 'it offered access to the everyday, the place where things are actually done, the sphere of practice that even in its most awkward and inept articulations makes a claim that is denied to the most eloquent of literary texts'.[12] It is upon this very ground, what Gallagher and Greenblatt call 'the everyday', that new historicism and cultural materialism begin to part ways.

One of the key distinctions between the two approaches would be much clearer if only Greenblatt's preferred name for his practice had stuck.[13] Then, rather than having to bother with 'new historicism', we would instead be able to compare cultural materialism to cultural poetics – and, as Kiernan Ryan notes, 'the summons to pursue a *materialist* critique of culture, as opposed to establishing a cultural *poetics*, speaks volumes about the differences between these two styles of radical criticism'.[14] These names tell us that the practices they denote are concerned with culture as a whole, but that they disagree on how exactly that whole can be understood. Is culture to be analysed through a materialist lens, or interpreted via a model of poetics? Here, 'poetics' is meant in its broader sense to denote the study or analysis, not merely of poetry, but of the organizing principles of any literary form. By analogy, that analysis is applied in new historicism to culture itself, but the residue of its exclusive application to literature inevitably remains. This is revealing because it coincides with an important assumption made by new historicism: the idea that for analytical purposes the culture of the past can be understood as a text. At one level, this principle connects with the interest in anecdotes and neglected artefacts. As Gallagher and Greenblatt remark, 'the notion of culture as text has a further major attraction: it vastly expands the range of objects available to be read and interpreted'.[15] But a more significant explanation is also given: 'it carries the core hermeneutical presumption that one can occupy a position from which one can discover meanings that those who left traces of themselves could not have articulated'.[16] In effect, then, new historicists are reading the culture of the past as they would read a book, looking for meaning by examining, for example, the metaphors, inconsistencies and anxieties that they discover 'written' on the intellectual fabric of what has been preserved of that culture. Gallagher and Greenblatt admit that this approach is not perfect – what, they ask, 'happens to such phenomena as social rituals and structures of feeling when they are textualized?' – but for them the advantages outweigh the disadvantages.[17]

From one perspective, all this is not so very different from the cultural materialist approach. Indeed, Gallagher and Greenblatt's emphasis on uncovering meanings that those who left them could not have expressed is similar to Pierre Macherey's version of literary analysis, itself a touchstone for cultural materialism. Macherey advocates a critical approach that pays attention to what he calls '*the unconscious of the work* (not of the author)'.[18] The distinction between author and work is important in that it distinguishes Macherey's method from a psychoanalytical one: for him the unconscious of the work reveals not repressed human desire or hidden compulsion, but 'the unconscious which is history, the play of history beyond its edges, encroaching on those edges: this is why it is possible to trace the path which leads from the haunted work to that which haunts it'.[19] In other words, since it is embedded within the culture of its time the text cannot help but interact with the historical conditions of its production. Thus the text makes certain assumptions, for example by granting some ideas the status of 'common sense' and leaving others unsaid, and in doing so, if read closely, it *reveals* the gaps in ideology'.[20] But where Gallagher and Greenblatt read the past as a text, Macherey's references to the 'edges' of the text and to that which 'haunts' it demonstrate his divergence from the new historicist position. For him, there is something outside of the text that cannot be reduced to it, something that he calls 'history'.

Macherey's ideas have been particularly important for cultural materialism, and the notion that a text can reveal ideological gaps bears strong similarity to Sinfield's concept of 'faultlines', which he defines as moments when the 'criteria of plausibility' that a dominant social order use to sustain itself 'fall into contest and disarray'.[21] Both Macherey and Sinfield posit the sort of demystification I discussed in the previous chapter, and they suggest that texts can be understood as sites of contestation where ideologies struggle and clash. None of this needs to have been consciously identified by the author, but it can become very apparent to a reader who is repeatedly told by an authority figure – perhaps a critic, teacher or politician – that, for instance, 'this is what Shakespeare meant'. As Sinfield puts it, 'it is a key proposition of cultural materialism that the specific historical conditions in which institutions and formations organize and are organized by textualities must be addressed'.[22] Note here that there are texts and there are historical conditions: the two are not one and the same. At certain times, texts organize institutions, such as the institution of Shakespeare studies, and at certain times those institutions organize texts by attributing values and meanings to them. It is this interplay between text and world, including the world of literary criticism, that cultural materialism turns its attention to. As Sinfield points out, this 'insistence on the processes through which a text achieves its current estimation is the key move in cultural materialism, and a principle difference in emphasis from new historicism'.[23] These processes are historical and social rather than textual. Cultural materialists resist what amounts to the aestheticization of history, the consequence of which, Drakakis warns, is 'to bracket culture *and* art as spheres to be differentiated from instrumental reason'.[24] For cultural materialists, while textuality remains an important focus of their analysis, there will always be some element of reality that escapes the gravitational pull of the text. Thus the 'materialism' in 'cultural materialism' testifies to this rejection of all transcendental readings of literature – '"materialism" is opposed to "idealism": it insists that culture does not (cannot) transcend the material forces and relations of production'.[25]

The cultural materialist position on this issue was drawn out in a debate between Dollimore, Sinfield and Catherine Belsey. Belsey has sometimes been referred to as a cultural materialist, but she has been reluctant to align herself with the approach and her work tends to find more value in poststructuralism, particularly the work of Jacques Derrida and Jacques Lacan, than is usually the case in the cultural materialism of Dollimore and Sinfield.[26] Belsey's disagreements with cultural materialism are demonstrated in a 1989 essay that challenges Dollimore on the question of textuality by drawing attention to the following quotation from *Political Shakespeare*:

the mere thinking of a radical idea is not what makes it subversive: typically it is the context of its articulation: to whom, how many and in what circumstances; one might go further and suggest that not only does the idea have to be conveyed, it has also actually to be used to refuse authority *or* be seen by authority as capable and likely of being so used.[27]

Belsey's objection to this is that '"ideas" apparently have materiality only if they are in some not very clearly specified way *put into* practice, or *perceived as* able to be so'.[28] She is working instead with a model of textuality based on Derrida's concept of 'différance', in which meanings constantly differ and defer, subject as they are to the continual play of indeterminacy.[29] As Belsey puts it, by making this move 'we release as material for analysis the play of signification ... which [is] not a reflection of the struggle for power, but its location'.[30] While on the surface the examination of the 'play of signification' does not sound too far away from Sinfield's 'contest of the criteria of plausibility', the key difference is marked by Belsey's implication that cultural materialism understands texts not as sites of struggle but simply as records of political action that takes place outside the text in an untheorized 'real world'. In her view, for cultural materialism 'the real struggle is once again elsewhere'.[31]

Dollimore and Sinfield responded to this critique in a co-authored piece published the following year. They begin by admitting that the very name cultural materialism 'implied a determined radical politics', but insist that in their analysis the political content of a text is never simply reflective of circumstances outside that text.[32] In the first section of the essay, Dollimore is unequivocal: 'I don't believe that the real struggle is always elsewhere than in the text, though I do believe that many struggles are not textual ... I would rather say that most struggles involve a struggle in and for representation.'[33] There should be nothing surprising about this formulation; indeed, an emphasis upon 'the contexts of articulation' is present in the passage quoted from *Political Shakespeare*. Dollimore is effectively saying that 'différance' and signification are important, but they will only get us so far since 'dominant social formations can and do reconstitute themselves around the self-same contradictions that destabilize them'.[34] So while literary analysis certainly does play a part in the struggle for a more progressive politics, it will not solve anything in itself.

Dollimore offered an excellent example of this tendency to overestimate the power of textual analysis when he returned to the issue a decade later. Referring to what he calls 'wishful theory', Dollimore notes that poststructuralist criticism often works according to a formula that is just as removed from the world of lived experience as the New Critics ever were. Such wishful theory locates a subversive element within a dominant ideology, posits the imminent collapse of that ideology, congratulates itself and moves on. In one passage, Dollimore offers this memorable example, 'some queer theorists regard male heterosexuality (it's rarely, if ever, female heterosexuality) as so intrinsically insecure as to be always about to self-destruct under the pressure of the homosexuality it is repressing. Dream on.'[35] One might react to this by falling into nihilism and giving up criticism altogether, convinced that nothing can be done, at least from within the academy, to change things. Another response might be to produce material that pays lip-service to what Belsey calls, in a later work, 'the usual liberal commonplaces', and condemns Western imperialism, heterosexism, environmental exploitation and similar wrongs out of a need to defend English Literature from accusations of irrelevance.[36] A third possibility is to find a way of doing criticism that really does make a difference – to engage with Sinfield's 'what it is all for' question.[37] This is, of course, more easily said than done. What might a critical account of Shakespeare that 'makes a difference' actually look like?

Sinfield's contribution to the 1990 response to Belsey offers a solution. Where he sees Belsey as wanting to hold on to a discipline of English Literature that shares with new historicism a desire to preserve familiar textualist methodologies while expanding the scope of their application to non-canonical texts, Sinfield has no compunction in proposing that the whole institution of 'Englit.' be torn down:

Cultural materialism embarrasses Englit. ... by requiring knowledges and techniques that we scarcely know how to discover. These are in part the provinces of history and other social sciences ... which require handling more complex than the tidy poststructuralist formula that everything, after all, is a text.[38]

What Sinfield proposes is no more than the logical end of the project of cultural materialism: to investigate the 'institutions that organise textualities' and the 'contexts of articulation' of texts. There is no greater institution, no greater context, for textuality than the discipline of English Literature itself. For Sinfield, then, 'The text is always a site of cultural conflict, but it is never a self-sufficient site.'[39] So making a difference to the institution of English Literature via Shakespeare might, for example, look very like the three essays that Sinfield contributes to the second edition of *Political Shakespeare*. These pieces address the way that Shakespeare has been taught, performed and appropriated by both mainstream and academic culture, and they each offer alternatives to the typically right-wing idealist accounts that have hitherto circulated.[40] The essays very deliberately engage with 'a struggle in and for representation', both the way that Shakespeare's work itself is represented and the representation of various 'out-groups', such as gendered, sexual, racial, religious, national and other minorities within it. But this is never overstated; Sinfield ends the first of his contributions to the volume with the following: 'teaching Shakespeare's plays and writing books about them is unlikely to bring down capitalism, but it is a point for intervention'.[41] No one, least of all Dollimore and Sinfield, expects the work of cultural materialists to act as the sole catalyst of social and political change, and if it does come such change will not be easy. But real change does sometimes happen, institutions do sometimes crumble, and, as Sinfield suggests, 'no one can be sure that his or her efforts will not tilt a local balance, in one direction or another'.[42] At the very least, the cultural and educational significance of Shakespeare offers itself as a privileged point from which such interventions can be made.

This model of intervention in a world that cannot be reduced to textuality marks a clear boundary between new historicist and cultural materialist methodologies. Yet underlying this split over culture as text and culture as material is a shared lineage that goes beyond the theoretical big bang in literary studies. Remarkably, the work of the same individual inspired both new historicism and cultural materialism, although it is fair to say that his parentage (for it is a he) to the former approach is a little more fraught than it is to the latter. His account of culture and his reformulation of key Marxist ideas have proven indispensable to criticism, and they offer important ways of nuancing the account of cultural materialism that I have given so far. It is time to reveal the man behind the curtain: Raymond Williams.

'This is what Raymond Williams was showing us for thirty years'

Raymond Williams is probably the most important British critic of the second half of the twentieth century.[43] His work represents the richest and most influential engagement with left-wing political and critical theory produced by an anglophone writer and, from the publication of his first essay in 1947 until his death in 1988, Williams strove to engage with literature in a politically committed and theoretically informed manner. The debts owed to him by cultural materialists and new historicists have not gone unacknowledged. This is abundantly clear in the case of cultural materialism since the phrase itself is Williams's own, 'borrowed', as Dollimore and Sinfield put it, for their related critical project.[44] Yet Greenblatt too has written about the influence of Williams, whom he encountered during a sojourn as a Fulbright scholar in 1960s Cambridge, where Williams taught. Greenblatt reflects that

> in Williams's lectures all that had been carefully excluded
> from the literary criticism in which I had been trained – who

controlled access to the printing press, who owned the land
and the factories, whose voices were being repressed as well
as being represented in literary texts, what social strategies
were being served by the aesthetic values we constructed –
came pressing back in upon the act of interpretation.[45]

As the quotation suggests, Williams was one of the first
literary critics to pay attention to the conditions within
which a text was produced and received, and this at a time
when the formalism of the New Critics dominated the
literary scene. While there is not the space to offer more than
a brief engagement with his work, in this section I consider
the nature of the debts owed by cultural materialism and
new historicism to Williams. I devote particular attention
to, first, his ideas about the relationship between culture and
the means of production, especially his reformulation of the
Marxist base and superstructure model, and, second, to what
he called residual, dominant and emergent cultural forms.

Williams's work is perhaps best characterized as a series
of fruitful clashes between literary criticism and Marxism;
as John Higgins notes, 'if we see his vocation as, in the first
instance, that of a socialist literary critic, then we can read
that commitment as riven by a conflict between its two
main components'.[46] The developments that that conflict
took over the course of Williams's career are complex,
but can be summed up as an initial allegiance to Marxist
literary criticism, followed by a period of disillusionment,
itself followed by an ultimate rapprochement predicated
upon Williams's reworking of some fundamental Marxist
positions. Williams writes that as a left-wing critic he felt
'exceptionally isolated' during the 1940s and 1950s, and
while he agreed with many Marxist positions in that period
he was nevertheless 'carrying on my own cultural and
literary work and inquiry at a certain conscious distance'.[47]
For this part of his career, Williams was essentially working
his way out of what was called 'vulgar Marxism'. From a
literary critical point of view, vulgar Marxism (also known as

orthodox Marxism or vulgar materialism) was problematic because it posited what came to be seen as a deterministic relationship between culture and economics. In this version of Marxism,

> no cultural activity is allowed to be real and significant in itself, but is always reduced to a direct or indirect expression of some preceding or controlling economic content, or of a political content determined by an economic position or situation.[48]

In other words, the economic base of a society (its material conditions), or a political system that has developed as a direct consequence of that base, simply determines a cultural superstructure that is nothing more than a reflection of economic relations. Thus the complexity and specificity of any artwork can easily be ignored, and Marxist literary analysis becomes a quite straightforward, not to say dull, activity. Williams characterized this, in an early work, as 'a rigid methodology, so that if one wishes to study, say, a national literature, one must begin with the economic history with which the literature co-exists, and then put the literature to it, to be interpreted in its light'.[49] He sees this rigidity as a consequence of the uncritical acceptance of the base/superstructure model itself, a model that Williams represents as hardening through misuse from a materialist observation into an idealist dogma. 'What is fundamentally lacking', writes Williams, 'is any adequate recognition of the indissoluble connections between material production, political and cultural institutions and activity, and consciousness'.[50]

Williams goes on to define these indissoluble connections more clearly when he turns his attention to resolving the limitations of the vulgar Marxist 'reflective' model of literary criticism in the final section of *Marxism and Literature*. He begins by discussing two tendencies in literary analysis: the formalist and the expressivist. For reasons that will be familiar from my discussion in Chapter 1, Williams has no faith in formalist literary analyses.

Nor does he see any value in the expressivist tendency typified by the kind of realist character analyses practised by A. C. Bradley. Williams rejects both approaches and arrives instead at a position in which literature is not reflective at all; instead, it plays an active role in the society of which it is a part. Referring to these two approaches, he remarks:

> the errors of each tendency are complementary, and can be corrected only by a fully social theory of literature. For the [written] notations are relationships, expressed, offered, tested, and amended in a whole social process, in which device, expression, and the substance of expression are in the end inseparable.[51]

In Williams's formulation literature is not removed to another ideal plane separate from the situation of the culture in which it exists, and nor can its content, form or underlying assumptions be divorced from that context. Instead, literature is implicated in complex relationships with its society, relationships that Williams calls 'productive', as opposed to reflective, because they actually produce responses to the historical conditions within which they have been written. Williams thus emphasizes the 'production (rather than only the reproduction) of meanings and values by specific social formations ... the centrality of language and communication as formative social forces, and ... the complex interaction both of institutions and forms and of social relationships and formal conventions'.[52] Williams called his solution to this problem 'cultural materialism', a term he first used in a 1976 essay that laid the groundwork for the following year's *Marxism and Literature*.[53] As Higgins puts it, for Williams 'the task of a cultural materialism was to attend to that constitutive role of signification within cultural process, and so to seek to integrate the three usually separated dimensions of textual, theoretical and historical analysis'.[54] A direct line can be drawn from this formulation to Sinfield's emphasis on examining 'institutions and formations [that] organize and are organized by textualities', and to the foundational definition of Dollimore and Sinfield's version of cultural materialism given in *Political Shakespeare*: 'a combination of historical context, theoretical method, political commitment and textual analysis'.[55] Gallagher and Greenblatt's summation of Williams's method again testifies to the facility of his approach for new historicists: '[he] did not read literature as the direct expression of otherwise forgotten mentalities, but rather as the record of submerged, semi-conscious structures. He read literature as the history of what hadn't quite been said.'[56]

If literature is to be understood as having a productive effect upon culture, a new, more nuanced model of culture is itself required to account for those effects. The very thing that models of culture like Tillyard's lacked was the capacity to account for ideas that dissented from what was erroneously supposed to be the ideological status quo. For example, as I demonstrated in Chapter 1, Tillyard has difficulty dealing with the way that the king challenges the dominant ethos of order and degree in *King Henry V* precisely because his model of culture has no way of incorporating such a challenge. Williams offered a solution to this problem by identifying two other cultural forms in addition to the dominant: the residual and the emergent. He defines the former as that element of a culture that

has been effectively formed in the past, but it is still active in the cultural process, not only and often not at all as an element of the past, but as an effective element of the present. Thus certain experiences, meanings, and values which cannot be expressed or substantially verified in terms of the dominant culture, are nevertheless lived and practised on the basis of the residue ... of some previous social and cultural institution or formation.[57]

Williams distinguishes the latter, emergent, element of the cultural process as 'new meanings and values, new practices, new relationships and kinds of relationship'.[58] These formulations provide a conceptual lens through which to understand and evaluate subversion; they allow, in effect, such subversion to be perceived more clearly than before. Which is not to say that such perception is now straightforward. Williams points out that the residual is easier to spot because it relates to pre-existing 'phases of the cultural process', while it can be very difficult to work out if a new cultural form is truly emergent or simply a 'merely novel' version of the dominant; none the less, in either case a deep understanding of history is necessary to allow such distinctions to be made in the first place.[59] The concept is further nuanced by his suggestion that the emergent and residual forms, while subordinate to the dominant ideology, may not necessarily be in conflict with it. In many cases, notes Williams, the residual 'has been wholly or largely incorporated into the dominant culture', and he gives the example of religion:

> organized religion is predominantly residual, but within this there is a significant difference between some practically alternative and oppositional meanings and values (absolute brotherhood, service to others without reward) and a larger body of incorporated meanings and values (official morality, or the social order of which the other-worldly is a separated neutralising or ratifying component).[60]

The spectre of Tillyard's work is again exorcized in Williams's final bracketed clause and replaced with a complexity that does not lend itself to monolithic concepts like a 'world-picture'. Instead, Williams leaves us with a version of culture that is riven with subtle, and not so subtle, ideological conflicts and where it is likely that a thousand dispiriting compromises occur for every truly radical break from the status quo. The categories 'alternative' and 'oppositional' allow the critic further scope for evaluation: is a subculture a fairly unthreatening alternative to the dominant ideology – say, vegetarianism in a habitually meat-eating country – or in provocative opposition to it, such as a pro-democracy movement in a dictatorship? As Sinfield acknowledges, Williams's most important contribution was to show that culture is neither single nor simple:

> we should expect the co-occurrence of subordinate, residual, emergent, alternative, and oppositional cultural mores alongside the dominant, in varying relations of incorporation, negotiation and resistance. The dominant may tolerate, repress, or incorporate subordinate formations, but that will be a continuous, urgent, and often strenuous project.[61]

Nevertheless, Williams's model of the cultural process is only a starting point. The real work of analysis exists in understanding, if possible, where cultural artefacts and practices fit into this schema.

The complexities and possibilities inherent in Williams's model can be demonstrated with a brief return to *Henry V* and, in particular, to a speech given by the Duke of Exeter at the closing stages of the battle of Agincourt. The speech describes the deaths of the Duke of York and the Earl of Suffolk:

> Suffolk died first, and York, all haggled over,
> Comes to him, where in gore he lay insteeped,
> And takes him by the beard, kisses the gashes
> That bloodily did yawn upon his face,
> He cries aloud 'Tarry, dear cousin Suffolk!
> My soul shall thine keep company to heaven.
> ...'
> So did he turn, and over Suffolk's neck
> He threw his wounded arm and kissed his lips,
> And so, espoused to death, with blood he sealed
> A testament of noble-ending love.
>
> (4.6.11–16, 24–7)[62]

Here we have a report of a passionate deathbed encounter between two aristocratic men that, to a twenty-first-century

reader, appears to carry erotic undertones. Is this an example
of the dominant, the residual or the emergent form of culture?
If either of the latter two, is it alternative or oppositional? To
give evidence that it is part of the dominant, I might point to
Thomas Elyot's *The Book Named the Governor* and Henry
Peacham's *The Compleat Gentleman*, two conduct manuals
that encourage elite men to enter into deep friendships with
other men of their status as a way of enforcing and extending
the power of their class.[63] Or I might turn to Alan Bray's
account of the heartfelt embraces shared between James I
and his court favourites as a way of indicating favour.[64] Yet
the practice is clearly a residual form too, as the classical
and medieval traditions of perfect friendship amply testify.[65]
Similarly, Alan Bray reveals that echoes of the eleventh-century
Catholic rites of sworn brotherhood, in which two men and
their families were linked together in a religious ceremony
akin to marriage, could be heard well into the early modern
period.[66] However, a case could be made for reading the
York–Suffolk encounter as an example of an emergent form
by extrapolating from Bruce R. Smith's argument that, in the
sonnets, 'Shakespeare improvised a new form of discourse. It
will not do to say that Shakespeare's sonnets cannot be about
homosexual desire since no one else in early modern England
addressed homosexual desire in just these terms.'[67] Perhaps
what Shakespeare discovered in the sonnets could be applied
to *Henry V*? And to show how all this might be oppositional to
the dominant I need only recall the way that same-sex desire is
punished in Christopher Marlowe's *Edward II*, the executions
of the king's favourites Bushy and Green, who are said to have
'Broke the possession of a royal bed / ... by your foul wrongs',
in Shakespeare's *King Richard II* (3.1.13, 15), and Francis
Bacon's concern that if a king has friends 'they purchase it
many times at the hazard of their own safety and greatness'.[68]
It is no easy matter to choose between these positions, each of
which can be supported with convincing historical evidence.

Sinfield comments on this speech twice, first in 1992 and
again in 2006, and what he does with it is perhaps surprising.

In the first piece, an extension of an essay written with Dollimore for *Alternative Shakespeares*, attention is drawn to the disturbing forces unleashed in *Henry V* by gender and sexuality. Dollimore and Sinfield focus on the fear of effeminacy that haunts both English and French soldiers, arguing that 'unmanliness' is not associated in this period with male–male passion but with 'regression towards the female'; nevertheless, they continue, 'same-sex passion, when sufficiently committed to masculine warrior values, is admired, even at the point where it slides towards the feminine'.[69] Bearing in mind Dollimore's point about wishful theory, a deconstructivist might argue that here, within the very bosom of the patriarchy, we find the hidden homoerotic other that will precipitate its downfall. Alternatively, laudably and even less interestingly, the passage could be used as a way of claiming that Shakespeare himself possessed an enlightened and refreshingly modern view of gender and sexuality – a claim that serves no other purpose than to reinvigorate Shakespeare's role as cultural totem from a progressive rather than reactionary position. In the 1992 piece, Dollimore and Sinfield suggest none of the above, instead pointing out that, while the eroticized tenderness between Suffolk and York is treated with respect by the play, the description of the two men ultimately does nothing to undermine the dominant ideology. After all, a few lines later King Henry orders the execution of the French prisoners – one of the most brutal acts of the entire play – and repeatedly emphasizes conventional masculinity in his marriage negotiations. Overall, they argue, 'the dominance of masculine attributes is represented as "order", and the answer when that order fails to carry conviction is said to be more order (rulers should be more manly)'. A closing statement deploys Williams's terminology: 'the dominant, characteristically, takes from its others what it can incorporate, leaving the remainder more decisively repudiated'.[70] It seems clear, then, that Dollimore and Sinfield's view is that any alternative or oppositional cultural forms associated with masculinity in the play, be they residual or emergent, are contained and dismissed. However, this fails to chime with a point made earlier in the same essay: 'the text is implicated, necessarily, in the complexities of its culture, and manifests not only the strategies of power but also the anxieties that protrude through them, making it possible always to glimpse alternative understandings'.[71] According to this interpretation, the dominant does not have things all its own way. In the 2006 piece, Sinfield places more emphasis on this subversion of dominant masculinity in the play. He reads the Suffolk and York speech as an example of excessive behaviour, and comments, 'manly same-gender devotion *may* betray an excess that hints at both effeminacy and dissident sexuality'.[72] Henry's execution of the prisoners is also understood a little differently. Now, while just as brutal, the act is a riskier, perhaps even futile gesture: 'masculinity is restored, but in a desperate way'.[73]

My aim here is not to point out that the interests and emphases of critics change over time – of course they do. Rather, I want to show just how hard it can be to establish the ideological position of a text, and also to suggest that, actually, there is nothing wrong with tentative readings. It seems to me very difficult to say whether the excessive behaviour recounted in the speech offers an alternative but non-threatening version of masculinity, whether it sets up a clear opposition to the dominant, or whether the dominant is able to contain the challenge that it faces. The key word in Sinfield's later analysis is 'may'. On balance, and more clearly in the 2006 reading, it appears there could well be something in the kisses and cries of York that disturbs the conventional model of upper-class male friendship, but in isolation it poses little threat to the dominant culture. That kind of nuance is available to a model of criticism that is possessed of the careful vocabulary of culture offered by Williams. By not claiming too much for this passage, Sinfield avoids what he later calls 'the *affirmative habit* of literary criticism' in which 'the critic will indulge in whatever strenuous reading is necessary to get the Shakespearean text onto his or her side'.[74]

Like Dollimore, Sinfield is concerned about the 'wishfulness' of some types of contemporary theory. And they are right to be concerned: literary criticism is full of the claims Sinfield alludes to, not least because competition for research funding and publication contracts encourages academics to inflate their findings with unprecedented amounts of hyperbole. Sinfield's 'may' is a way of arresting that trend; it is a modest proposal made in the interest of keeping debate about Shakespeare open rather than unquestioningly allotting him a position on the political right or left. Such openness can come as a surprise to readers who have been led to believe that cultural materialists, who unfailingly espouse left-wing causes, continually discover a 'right-on' Shakespeare who acts as a cheerleader for their radical beliefs. This misunderstanding may be the result of a long-running debate between new historicists and cultural materialists that, in the end, generated more heat than light. Its starting point was the model of culture offered by Williams, and its object was the political direction of Greenblatt's work and new historicism in general. The debate posed a very straightforward question: 'just how politically radical are new historicism and cultural materialism?' As is often the case, that simple question produced a very complicated answer.

The subversion/containment debate

The argument goes like this: new historicists – American, earnest, liberal – read Shakespeare and other early modern texts for evidence of subversion, but find only containment. Meanwhile, cultural materialists – British, provocative, socialist – set out to find subversion, and succeed where their colleagues across the pond have failed. It is thus demonstrated that new historicists are less politically radical than cultural materialists. There is an element of truth in this caricature: cultural materialists do tend to be provocative British socialists keen on highlighting subversion in the culture of the past and the present, and new historicists typically take a little more convincing. From the American Don E. Wayne's perspective,

> At the present moment in Britain it is difficult to locate oneself within the field of Shakespeare studies without at the same time acknowledging the coordinates of one's position, not only in the territory of academic politics but in the larger political domain as well ... In America, on the other hand, ever since Eliot and the New Critics established the principle of aesthetic distance ... as a *sine qua non* of literary study, we have tended to repress the political nature of our activity as critics.

This is a devilishly exciting model for British academics – and perhaps British people in general – who, for once, are thought to be much less repressed than their American counterparts. Wayne even describes British cultural materialists as 'freewheeling' in an earlier paragraph.[75] And there is an appeal for US critics here too; as Belsey points out, by rejecting Tillyard and his ilk American new historicists 'had no further call to locate authority on the other side of the Atlantic'.[76] Nevertheless, despite their appeal it would be unfair to suggest that these distinctions remain hard and fast, since over the course of their careers new historicists like Greenblatt and Gallagher have not foreclosed the possibility of genuine subversion, and cultural materialists like Dollimore and Sinfield have demonstrated a full awareness of the difficulties of achieving it. The cultural materialist side of this debate was rehearsed in Dollimore and Sinfield's account of *Henry V* discussed in Chapter 1, where they argue that at first the play seems to neutralize the subversive forces it represents via 'aesthetic colonization', but ultimately, they decide, in representing such challenges the play renders the dominant available for demystification.[77] Again we see the openness that was present in Sinfield's later reading of the same play above, together with the acknowledgement that another, less optimistic, interpretation may be available. Apart from the appeal of the caricature and the pigeonhole, what in fact seems to have caused the hardening of these myths about new historicists and cultural materialists is the misreading of an early essay by Greenblatt, and in particular, of the eleven-word sentence with which he ended it.

'Invisible Bullets' is one of Greenblatt's most successful and popular pieces. It was much in demand during the 1980s, was printed, albeit in slightly different versions, in no less than four publications between 1981 and 1988, and addressed directly the question of subversion and containment.[78] With reference to a 1588 book by Thomas Harriot, an Elizabethan man of science, entitled *A Brief and True Report of the New Found Land of Virginia*, the first part of the essay shows how even atheism – one of the most subversive ideas of the era – could be co-opted by the dominant as a means of enacting power. In his book, Harriot relates what occurred when, as part of the first English colony in the Americas, he and his countrymen encountered the native Algonkian people. Harriot's observations about religion are particularly interesting, as he comes to see that by encouraging the Algonkians to fear the Christian God, the Europeans can control them much more easily than with brute force alone. Religion is thus used as a means of social manipulation, and this practice prompts the thought, already circulated by Machiavelli, that all religion amounts to little more than crowd control. Greenblatt's point is that this realization of the social utility of religion is only possible at all as part of the exercise of European colonial power, and indeed it works to bolster the very power that it might have been thought to subvert. As he puts it:

Thus the subversiveness which is genuine and radical – sufficiently disturbing so that to be suspected of such beliefs could lead to imprisonment and torture – is at the same time contained by the power it would appear to threaten. Indeed, the subversiveness is the very product of that power and furthers its ends. One may go still further and suggest that the power Harriot both serves and embodies not only produces its own subversion but is actively built upon it.[79]

Greenblatt then moves to the second tetralogy, suggesting that, like the radical view of religion produced by the English colonists, any subversive potential that might be manifested by, say, Falstaff 'proves to be utterly bound up with Hal, contained politically by his purposes'.[80] Indeed, Hal's own playful theatricality, visible most memorably in the tavern scenes of *Henry IV, Part 1* but running throughout his character, suggests to Greenblatt that theatricality itself 'is not set over against power but is one of power's essential modes'.[81] The essay ends with the fateful words 'there is subversion, no end of subversion, only not for us'.[82]

Objections to the supposed political quietism of new historicism soon saw their way into print. Carolyn Porter offers an excellent and representative account of the kind of criticism 'Invisible Bullets' encountered. Drawing attention to the logic underlying Greenblatt's assertion that the theatrical is thoroughly aligned with power, she argues:

If theatricality, or literature, or art in general, is under-stood as *either* 'set over against power' *or* 'one of power's essential modes,' and if this either/or allies the first choice with a formalist belief in literature's autonomy, then only formalists can believe that literature might harbour any socially resistant or oppositional force. Meanwhile, to believe that literature might have social or political weight as a form of cultural agency entails also believing that such agency as it has is by definition already co-opted by 'power.' What is thus excluded is the possibility that literature might well – at least occasionally – act as an oppositional cultural agent in history.[83]

This formulation describes a classic Catch-22 situation: either the theatre is capable of opposition but exists in a separate aesthetic realm and therefore cannot enact that opposition, or it is capable of agency in the world but cannot foment opposition because it has always already been enlisted by power. With critiques like this, it is easy to see why new historicism developed a reputation for timidity, especially when this seemingly inevitable containment is contrasted with far sexier cultural materialist views contemporary with Greenblatt's. Take Steven Mullaney (an American), who writes on the same topic but arrives at the opposite conclusion. For him, Shakespeare's theatre is located in an area of London 'traditionally reserved for cultural phenomena that could not be contained within the strict or proper bounds of the community', and therefore predisposed to offer 'a performance *of* the threshold, by which the horizon of community was made visible, the limits of definition, containment and control made manifest'.[84] Mullaney's point is persuasive. Located on the south bank of the river Thames beyond the jurisdiction of the municipal authorities and a short walk away from brothels and bear-baiting arenas, the Globe Theatre does not immediately suggest itself as a bastion of state power. Of course, what takes place upon the stage might attempt to reformulate the relationship between the physical and ideological location of the theatre, but it is surely just as possible that it might not. This possibility is key: if critics of Shakespeare begin to suggest that the radical potential of his work is always contained or never contained, then we may as well all go back to being Tillyardians. As Porter notes, 'the solution ... is not to substitute subversion for domination, out of some political conviction that the oppressed will overcome, but to frame the discourse under consideration in such a way as to include sufficient discursive evidence' to arrive at a reasonable conclusion either way.[85] This is echoed by Dollimore:

> just as containment theorists should not judge a priori that all subversion is contained, so its opponents cannot decide a priori that all power structures are subvertible; each instance, if it can be decided at all, can only be done so historically.[86]

Since the flashpoint of the late 1980s, all the leading players in new historicism and cultural materialism have acknowledged

that the subversion/containment debate, certainly with regard
to Greenblatt's work and when used as a sort of spotters'
guide to political criticism of Shakespeare, did more to close
down thought than open it up. The notorious phrase 'no end
of subversion, only not for us', borrowed from Kafka, was
perhaps too axiomatic for its own good. While I think Porter's
objection to Greenblatt's concept of theatricality is correct, in
that final sentence of 'Invisible Bullets' he was, in fact, making
an argument about criticism and ideology, not the radical
potential of drama. His point, clearer in the penultimate and
rarely quoted sentence, was that the subversive elements of
Shakespeare plays are easier for contemporary readers to spot
because, for us, historical distance and ideological change has
taken the sting out of them. Greenblatt writes, 'we are free to
locate and pay homage to the plays' doubts only because they
no longer threaten us'.[87] In Dollimore's words, 'the return of
the repressed is a welcome topic for political critique when
it is someone else's repression and not threatening to us'.
Dollimore then goes on to quote the 'no end of subversion'
line that he notes 'Greenblatt notoriously and rightly said in
another context'.[88] Similarly, Sinfield remarks that Greenblatt
'is in my view right to say that his "Invisible Bullets" essay
has often been misinterpreted'.[89] For his part, on the subject
of whether sites of resistance are always co-opted by the
dominant, Greenblatt has simply remarked 'some are, some
aren't'.[90] It is therefore difficult not to concur with Montrose,
who argues that the opposition between containment and
subversion is 'so reductive, polarized and undynamic as to
be of little or no conceptual value'.[91] One rather dispiriting
explanation for the longevity of these unhelpful caricatures is
presented by Dollimore: 'the often remarked differences have
had more to do with the professional need to classify and
process than with what's interesting about the perspectives'.[92]
As I have tried to show in this chapter, while there certainly
are points of difference between new historicism and cultural
materialism, it is tedious and counterproductive to exaggerate
them. What matters for cultural materialism is not dogmatic

allegiance to a set methodology, but an openness to the 'may' that neither arbitrarily limits the radical possibilities of Shakespeare's work nor wishfully overestimates them.

3

State vs Individual: Cultural Materialism and Agency

To be or not to be

What might Hamlet mean by the phrase 'to be, or not to be'?
The question is surprisingly difficult to answer despite, or
perhaps because of, the fact that these words appear in the
best-known line of dramatic verse Shakespeare ever wrote.
The quotation is so familiar that it is difficult in the twenty-
first century even to hear or read it properly. For example,
a very capable student of mine once opened an essay on
Hamlet with the claim that 'to be or not to be' represented
the 'most famous five words' in the English language. I gently
pointed out that there were either six words in the quotation
or, discounting repetition, four. Outside of academia, more
often than not the words are used as a simple catchphrase
to be placed alongside 'Beam me up, Scotty', 'Do you feel
lucky, punk?' and the immortal 'You're only supposed to
blow the bloody doors off!' In casual conversation, these
lines often indicate nothing more than a, sometimes cursory,
familiarity with the source texts from which they originate,
and a desire to demonstrate a level of cultural proficiency that

will gain approbation. As Terence Hawkes has pointed out, 'bits of [*Hamlet*'s] language embed themselves in everyday speech until it starts to seem like a web of quotations'.[1] Given Shakespeare's preeminent place in English-speaking culture, quoting the most famous line from his most famous play might well be thought to garner a significant amount of cultural capital. And as we have seen, it is on occasions such as this that the ears of the cultural materialist prick up, because it is always worth paying attention to what happens when the meaning of Shakespeare's words is neglected in favour of the cultural power they enact. But for a phrase that can often refer to little more than Shakespeare's cultural power, 'to be or not to be' is itself curiously unemphatic. Unlike most popular Shakespearean quotations, including those discussed in Chapter 1, it cannot be said to offer much in the way of wisdom. Nor, like the pop culture quotations above, is it about taking immediate action. Rather, the line encapsulates a moment in which wisdom and action come to rest and self-examination takes over. Little wonder, then, that in a world that cannot bear very much philosophy, when quoted the phrase is often reworked to make the terms of Hamlet's question more concrete. Recent examples of this include 'to buy or not to buy?', 'to breed or not to breed?' and 'to vape or not to vape?' Alternatively, the phrase is followed by words that clarify its meaning, such as 'to be or not to be an entrepreneur?' The answers to some of these questions will be more straightforward than others, but in each case they studiously avoid addressing the issue that Hamlet is interested in: what might it mean 'to be or not to be'?

As scholars have recognized, the unprecedented space allocated to such enquiries in Shakespeare's *Hamlet* is one of the qualities that distinguishes the play from its precursors. In the words of Jonathan Bate, it is 'Hamlet's extreme self-consciousness which sets him apart from the traditional revenger'.[2] Nevertheless, 'To be, or not to be' (3.1.55)[3] is a strikingly abstract way of putting things even for a play that is interested in addressing the question of vengeance from an ethical perspective. The word 'be' has caused all the trouble. Hamlet is clearly asking a question about existence or 'being', but what that question actually is continues to be debated.[4] Some critics suggest that the words show Hamlet is contemplating suicide, and thus that 'be' should be understood in the sense of 'remain alive'. Hamlet certainly does ponder suicide, but not until later in the speech when he talks about bearing 'those ills we have' rather than killing oneself and thus flying 'to others that we know not of' (3.1.80–1). Other readings advocate a less practical outlook at this early point in the speech, and argue Hamlet is thinking in a more philosophical vein by weighing up the benefits of living or never having lived at all. A third interpretation understands 'be', slightly less literally, to mean 'act', specifically against Claudius, and in doing so appeals to the lines that follow for support:

To be, or not to be – that is the question;
Whether 'tis nobler in the mind to suffer
The slings and arrows of outrageous fortune
Or to take arms against a sea of troubles
And by opposing end them.

(3.1.55–9)

Here Hamlet immediately glosses the first line of the speech by counterpointing inaction with action. This reading might at first seem to move the question away from the philosophical and back to the practical, positioning Hamlet's dilemma as a struggle between bravery and cowardice. And these terms are in fact used later in the speech when Hamlet remarks that 'conscience does make cowards – ' (3.1.82). But to read Hamlet as asking a question about action does not necessarily mean having to abandon philosophy. Indeed, this passage can be understood in the terms of its time as a central dilemma in the philosophy of stoicism.[5] Yet the speech engages just as closely with modern philosophical debates, specifically those that took place in post-Second World War Europe and that had a significant effect upon the formulation and reception of cultural materialism. These debates, prompted chiefly by the work of Michel Foucault and Louis Althusser, pondered the same question asked by Hamlet in the 'to be, or not to be' speech, and indeed by the play as a whole: what are the conditions and limits of human action?

In this chapter, I will examine cultural materialist attitudes to individual agency, especially as they relate to the power of the state. This is an issue of some importance for three reasons. First, as I've shown, cultural materialist readings almost always orient themselves around the potential subversion of or dissent from an establishment position. The establishment might take many forms in the past or the present – it could be the Elizabethan state, the A level exam board or the Royal Shakespeare Company – but a key question in each discussion is the degree to which individuals are able to resist the power that is exerted upon them. As the subversion/containment debate shows, this is a complex question. Second, misunderstanding the position of cultural materialism on human agency risks misunderstanding cultural materialism itself. If the cultural materialist approach is dismissed as 'just another postmodern theory', it is all too easy to miss the distinctive contribution it makes to criticism on the very subject of action-in-the-world. As a corollary, and third, the position of cultural materialism on human agency has indeed been regularly misunderstood. To set things right, I will engage with a recent example of one such misunderstanding and suggest how it might have arisen. In a later speech, Hamlet warns against 'thinking too precisely on th'event' (4.4.40); nevertheless, precise thinking about agency is necessary if cultural materialism is to claim any efficacy for its methodology and not 'lose the name of action' (3.1.87).

In 2013, Jonathan Dollimore reviewed two books by Neema Parvini in the journal *Textual Practice*. The books, *Shakespeare's History Plays: Rethinking Historicism* and *Shakespeare and Contemporary Theory: New Historicism and Cultural Materialism* (both 2012), addressed the legacy of the theoretical innovations I discussed in Chapter 2. As Parvini's work is notable for its robust critiques of new historicism and cultural materialism, the editors of the journal may well have anticipated fireworks when they commissioned Dollimore's review. They were not to be disappointed. In a ten-page rebuttal, Dollimore takes Parvini to task for what he calls 'elementary errors ... which need to be remarked on because they are shared by many others'.[6] Several of Dollimore's criticisms are phrased in this inclusive manner ('like many others', 'Parvini and many others', 'the reductive orthodoxy ... perpetuated in the secondary literature'), but otherwise few punches are pulled. Parvini replied to Dollimore's review in equally combative mode, and while conceding that some criticisms can be accounted for by the fact that studies like his 'which range over a vast field, are prone by necessity to making some neat elisions', for the most part he rejects Dollimore's points.[7] Dollimore is given the last word in a response to Parvini's reply. In drawing attention to this debate I do not wish to wallow in disagreement: nobody likes receiving bad reviews, and writing them is almost as dispiriting. But the role of human agency in cultural materialism is one of the key grounds on which this exchange takes place, and as such it offers an excellent opportunity to examine the claims made on either side.

Parvini's central objection to the cultural materialist method is that it presents an incoherent view of the relationship between ideology and human agency. He detects what he sees as a flagrant contradiction at the core of the approach: if, as he suggests, cultural materialists understand human behaviour not as the exercise of free will but instead as nothing other than the effect of ideological pressures, how can they themselves claim to escape such pressures when offering their own critiques? In *Shakespeare and Contemporary Theory*, Parvini puts it like this:

How can cultural materialism be po-facedly and militantly against essentialist humanism and committed to theorists, such as Althusser and Foucault who ... have no place for the autonomous free-thinking individual in their systems of control, *and* argue for a critical practice of *subjectivity*? Where is this magical subjectivity coming from? Is it not just the 'culture' or 'ideology' that made you and to which you are entirely subjected, reflected back on that same culture or ideology? ... These sorts of questions appear to have no answer and the tension between anti-humanism and 'subjective' criticism strikes me as being hopelessly contradictory.[8]

At base this is an objection to, as Parvini sees it, having one's anti-essentialist (and anti-humanist) cake and eating it too. These are serious charges, strongly put. Setting the accusation of po-facedness to one side for the moment, there are three separate claims here: that cultural materialism is anti-essentialist and anti-humanist; that it is committed to the 'systems of control' of Althusser and Foucault; and that its critical practice is one of 'subjectivity'. For the sake of clarity, I will address each of these points in turn.

Anti-essentialism and anti-humanism

In referring to the topics of anti-essentialism and anti-humanism, Parvini invokes a vast hinterland of philosophical debate stretching across continents and centuries that it is impossible to do full justice to here. Nevertheless, a useful starting point would be to ask whether Parvini is correct in attributing these tendencies to cultural materialism. The short answer (as so often) is yes and no: Parvini is right that cultural materialism is anti-essentialist, but wrong that it is anti-humanist. Dollimore devotes a substantial portion of his review to addressing this issue, pointing out that the terms anti-humanism and anti-essentialism are so misunderstood that he advocated abandoning them altogether as long ago as the 1984 publication of *Radical Tragedy*.[9] As it is often impossible to fully understand ideas in isolation, in the

longer answer that follows I will touch upon a constellation
of positions, showing how they develop in relation to one
another.

Essentialism is the belief that all human beings contain
within them some sort of natural essence that infuses them
with the qualities that make them human. People of a religious
persuasion might call this a soul, while atheists might prefer
to use the term 'human nature'. These are idealist positions
because they rely not upon evidence but upon metaphysical
belief. It follows, then, that anti-essentialists reject these beliefs
on whatever grounds they are based, and take the position that
there is nothing innate in human beings; instead, they argue
that human identity, whatever it might actually be, proceeds
from human existence. This is a materialist way of thinking.
These ideas were most famously expressed by Jean-Paul Sartre
in the philosophy known as existentialism, which held the
phrase 'existence precedes essence' as a central tenet. Why
might cultural materialists and others wish to abandon essentialism? A chief reason, as Dollimore and Sinfield have pointed
out throughout their careers, is that it is all too easy for essen-
tialists to use a working definition of human nature to exclude
those who are considered not to fit the parameters that have
been defined. As Dollimore argues in *Radical Tragedy*,

> essentialism, rooted as it is in the concept of centred
> structure and determining origin, constitutes a residual
> metaphysic within secularist thought which, though it
> has not entailed has certainly made possible the classic
> ideological effect: a specific cultural identity is universalised
> or naturalised; more specifically, in reaction to social
> change this residual metaphysic is activated in defence of
> one cultural formation, one conception of what it is to be
> truly human, to the corresponding exclusion of others.[10]

universality is a dehumanising tool [handwritten marginal note]

The twentieth century offered a horrifying amount of evidence
for the accuracy of this judgement, and the twenty-first does
not seem likely to disprove it any time soon. Despite these

serious concerns, Dollimore is not so dogmatic as to dismiss essentialism out of hand. There are occasions, he points out, when it might prove a useful position to take: 'while some literary theorists deplore essentialism in all its forms, there is ample evidence of its historically progressive function for subordinate cultures'.[11] Dollimore alludes here to Gayatri Chakravorty Spivak's notion of 'strategic essentialism': the deployment of essentialist arguments for a specific political goal.[12] This is a good example of how undogmatic cultural materialism can be. Since it is an approach in which, as Sinfield puts it, 'the choice of reading modes is *strategic* ... governed by what seems likely to disclose the political potential of the text', a realignment of positions and allegiances is perfectly acceptable if it offers a way of achieving a progressive outcome.[13]

The term 'humanism' is if anything more complex than 'essentialism', and today is popularly used as a synonym for secularism. In an early modern context, it usually describes the European cultural movement probably best represented by the work of Erasmus and Thomas More. While the early modern humanists remained Christian, their knowledge of the achievements of ancient Greek and Roman writers encouraged them to put a far higher value on humanity than had previously been the case. This kind of Christian humanism was adopted by Tillyard and other critics of his era. However, when discussing contemporary philosophical positions humanism is more properly defined by its juxtaposition with theism, the belief in an interventionist God as source of goodness and guarantee of meaning in human affairs. The kind of humanists that Parvini and Dollimore are referring to replace that God with 'Man', more often than not an essentialist concept predicated once more upon the idea of a universal and innate human nature experienced by all. Rather than viewing history as the working out by God of his purpose on earth, humanists see events in the world as entirely within the control of human beings, and these events are often understood in the light of grand narratives such as 'human progress'. Humanism is generally optimistic in tone, and it emphasizes human achievements in the fields of art, literature and science, as well as broader values such as democracy, reason and compassion. Yet the kind of secular essentialist humanism thus described is not the only version of contemporary humanism available. In his review of Parvini's work, Dollimore points out that although Sartre's existentialism discarded the concept of universal human nature and was thus anti-essentialist, it clung nevertheless to a concept of 'a human universality of *condition*' that is defined as a state 'of being in the world, of having to labour and to die there'.[14] While it echoes the questions Hamlet was asking, this is of course a Marxist idea, encapsulated in the well-known phrase 'it is not the consciousness of men that determines their being, but, on the contrary, their social being that determines their consciousness'.[15] The notion of a human condition revealed through existence is a materialist position but it is one that, in so far as it posits a universally shared human condition, can be described as anti-essentialist humanism. Kate Soper offers a useful definition of this kind of humanism:

> it recognizes the historicity of human culture and the problems which it poses for any universalizing discourse about the 'human condition'. Emphasizing the situatedness of the individual within society, it rejects the 'isolated' individual invoked by liberal theory together with the contrast between the 'social' and the 'individual' which such a viewpoint imposes. At the same time, however, it insists that individuals are autonomous within society in the sense that it is their actions which lie at the source of what is social.[16]

The final sentence excepted, this definition would stand uncontroversially for a description of the cultural materialist approach to the relationship between the individual and society in history. Consider, for example, Sinfield: 'according to cultural materialism, our "humanity" is not an essential condition towards which we may aspire, but what people have as a consequence of being socialized into human communities'.[17] In its analysis of all kinds of texts, cultural materialism is concerned with, as Soper puts it, 'emphasizing the situatedness of the individual in society' at least in so far as the individual is defined here, and rejecting universalist ideas – although of course it also concerns itself with the way that texts find themselves used in social circumstances other than those that produced them. Nevertheless, Parvini would argue that Soper's final sentence above does not apply to cultural materialism, which, as we have seen, he suggests has 'no place for the autonomous free-thinking individual'. This is an accusation of anti-humanism.

Anti-humanists accept the secular basis of humanism in that they too remove God from their system, but they dissent from the idea that 'Man' can simply step into the central role vacated by the deity. This objection is not made out of pessimism or nihilism but is rather a judgement based upon a radical understanding of the ideological condition of being in the world. Taking one step beyond Sartre's position, anti-humanists argue for a model of humanity that must not only relinquish the concept of any kind of universal or fixed human nature, but also abandon the idea that humans have any influence over their historical circumstances at all. If anti-essentialists replace essence with existence and humanists replace God with 'Man', anti-humanists replace both of these concepts with visions of the human being ensnared by systems beyond his or her individual control. Why are some critics opposed to this anti-humanist position? An answer is offered by Soper in her account of one aspect of the terminological confusion to which Dollimore has alluded. She sees key elements of anti-humanism as having been lost in their translation from a French philosophical tradition to an Anglo-American one. In the latter tradition, anti-humanism is strongly associated with misanthropy and a rejection of the best aspects of human culture; hence, for some, anti-humanism is tantamount to barbarism. Soper notes that things look very different when seen from a continental perspective:

If we 'speak English', then, 'anti-humanism' amounts to a dogmatic rejection of the 'irenic and mediatory ethic'[18] which self-styled humanists have always deemed an essential component of their enlightenment. If we 'speak French', on the other hand, it constitutes itself a new enlightenment from whose purview every form of humanist thinking is revealed as no less obfuscatory and mythological than the theology and superstition which the 'humanist' movement has traditionally congratulated itself upon rejecting.[19]

From the tradition of French thought, humanism is thus a new form of idealism that has simply repackaged the type of mystification that was previously associated with the divine and rebranded it as human nature. The effect, in a famous phrase by Marx, is to 'resolve the essence of religion into the essence of *man*'.[20] It is tempting to think that criticism of anti-humanism might still carry with it the sort of dogmatism that exists in the anglophone interpretation of the concept. But of course Parvini offers other grounds for his rejection of anti-humanism that stem from his concern about what he sees as the weakened role of human agency in cultural materialism. In *Shakespeare's History Plays*, he accuses Dollimore and Sinfield of misrepresenting in their work the very tenet that they so often cite: 'men and women make their own history, but not in conditions of their own choosing'.[21] Parvini asks 'what would become of this in the hands of Dollimore and Sinfield? Their version might read: "social and political processes make history, under conditions of their own creation".'[22] Dollimore offers a brisk rebuttal of this accusation:

[Parvini] asks: 'Don't Dollimore and Sinfield assume that dissidence is the result of ideological contradiction rather than the result of individuals taking action?' Nope, we do not. However, we have argued that sometimes dissidence occurs through individuals acting in scenarios *made possible* by ideological contradictions.[23]

Of course, it is one thing to articulate a theoretical perspective and quite another to apply it, so since Parvini's claims are directed at the actual critical practice of Dollimore and Sinfield it is only fair to assess them in that arena.

Parvini's criticism of cultural materialist methodology, above, arises out of his analysis of the essay on *King Henry V* that I have previously discussed. He takes particular exception to an early passage in which Dollimore and Sinfield offer an alternative to three types of criticism that they see as deeply flawed: the Christian humanism of Tillyard, the nihilism of Jan Kott, and the insular humanism of Wilbur Sanders.[24] They point out that the 'fundamental error in all these accounts of the role of ideology is falsely to unify history and/or the individual human subject'.[25] I gave an example of this first point in Chapter 1 with reference to Tillyard, who offered a unifying ideological account of history based on the universal principle of order and degree. The second point, what Dollimore and Sinfield call the false unification of the individual human subject, is a reference to the essentialist and universalist conceptions of the human being that I have been discussing above. Each of the three critical positions they attack in this piece responds to the political injustice and upheaval represented by Shakespeare's histories and tragedies with a recipe for inaction: Tillyard sees unity in universal order and thus no need for political action; Kott sees unity in universal anarchy and thus no point in political action; and Sanders sees the same anarchy but advocates a withdrawal into the unified individual self. In a passage also quoted in part by Parvini, Dollimore and Sinfield offer a different approach. Crucially, this is an approach that gestures towards a model of political action:

> the alternative to this [unity] is not to become fixated on its negation – chaos and subjective fragmentation – but rather to understand history and the human subject in terms of social and political process. Ideology is composed of those beliefs, practices, and institutions that work to legitimate

the social order – especially by the process of representing sectional or class interests as universal ones. This process presupposes that there are other, subordinate cultures that, far from sharing the interests of the dominant one, are in fact being exploited by it. This is one reason why the dominant tend not only to 'speak for' the subordinate but actively to repress it as well. This repression operates coercively but also ideologically (the two are in practice inseparable). So, for example, at the same time that the Elizabethan ruling fraction claimed to lead and speak for all, it not only persecuted those who did not fit in, but even blamed them for social instability that originated in its own policies.[26]

Dollimore and Sinfield develop here an analytical methodology that is anti-essentialist and anti-universalist in so much as it relies upon a concept of the human being that is not self-creating and self-sufficient but instead is buffeted by ideological forces that are not of its own production or control. Those ideological forces have a material effect, and their aim is to shore up the status quo. In doing so they reveal that some elements of a culture are demonized, and it is through this revelation that political action can begin to be formulated. This action might take place at the level of the individual, but it is more likely to occur, and certainly more likely to succeed, on a collective basis.

For this reason, the theatre has a special place in early modern culture. As I mentioned in Chapter 2, its physical location beyond the control of the elders of the City of London allowed it to perform the role of sceptical inter-preter of official English culture and, moreover, to probe the ideological contradictions or faultlines that occurred in that culture. These faultlines emerge for ideological reasons, but they are put under pressure by human agents. As Dollimore and Sinfield argue in the paragraph following that quoted above, it is 'likely that the topics that engaged writers and audiences alike were those where ideology was under strain'.[27]

These topics, in other words, were chosen by human agents – writers – and seem to have proven of interest to other human agents – audiences. This formulation has the virtue of retaining the intrinsic complexity of social processes that was a key part of Raymond Williams's model of culture while also acknowledging that there is scope for individual responses that are not completely pre-determined. The point about agency is made again later in the essay when Dollimore and Sinfield sum up *Henry V* as a 'displaced, imaginary resolution of one of the state's most intractable problems': the subjugation of Irish rebels and the unification of the four kingdoms of Britain.[28] Here it is clear that in their account of the play there are human agents – Irish rebels – who can be contained neither by ideological nor by military means. Shakespeare's play, in part, attempts a fantastical version of that containment, but it remains nothing more than fantasy, and in the event the rebels succeeded in resisting Elizabethan attempts at repression.

Nevertheless, it is probably fair to say that the role of human agency is not as strongly emphasized in Dollimore and Sinfield's essay on *Henry V* as it is elsewhere in their work. This is probably because they are not particularly concerned with that aspect of their cultural materialist practice in this essay; their interest lies instead in the ways that the ambitions of a ruling culture come to be both legitimized and destabilized by Shakespeare's play. However, in a footnote they do draw attention to the fact that cultural materialism has more to say about ideology: 'a materialist criticism will be concerned with aspects of ideology additional to those dealt with here, and our emphasis on ideology as legitimation, though crucial, should not be taken as an exhaustive definition of the topic'.[29] Here Dollimore and Sinfield gesture towards a broader sense of ideology as prone to dissidence, a position that is developed more clearly in other texts. The footnote refers the reader to *Radical Tragedy* and *Political Shakespeare* but, as I will go on to show, important passages on this issue can also be found in *Faultlines* itself, in Sinfield's *Shakespeare, Authority, Sexuality* and in Dollimore's later work.

In his response to Dollimore's review, Parvini draws attention to a particular word in the long passage quoted above:

> I have deliberately emphasised the word 'work' here; it is a verb, an action that assumes, one would think, a doer. But the concept of 'individual human subjects' has just been discredited; there is no single person or even group of people responsible for this process; the 'beliefs, practices, and institutions' just *work* 'by themselves', in the abstract.[30]

The claim that cultural materialism discredits the concept of 'individual human subjects' goes to the heart of the accusations of anti-humanism that it has sometimes faced. I think this is a misreading. In the same passage, Dollimore and Sinfield advocate understanding 'the human subject in terms of social and political processes', as an alternative to the 'individual integrity' of the human subject favoured by humanist criticism. This is not the same as saying there are no individual subjects; the point is rather that individual subjects cannot remain unaffected by the social and political circumstances in which they find themselves (or, to take a psychoanalytical approach, by the vagaries of the human mind itself), and that ideology plays a significant part in organizing the way that an individual relates to those circumstances. Individual subjects do exist, but, as John Donne well knew, 'no man is an island, entire of itself; every man is a piece of the continent, a part of the main'.[31] Cultural materialism does not suggest that human agency is a myth; after all, one of the distinguishing features of the approach is its emphasis upon the 'what it is all for', or the capacity to use criticism, especially of Shakespeare, to intervene in the world beyond the page. As Sinfield says, far from rejecting the idea of human agency, 'cultural materialists were preoccupied with how to construct a model of cultural production that did *not* fall into the determinism that had influenced earlier Marxist theories'.[32]

But in the passage above Parvini asks a further question: if ideology is a material practice that has a significant effect upon actual human beings, why can't some other human beings be held responsible for it? And how can it be said to 'work by itself'? An answer to the first question is in fact offered by Dollimore and Sinfield in the quotation from *Faultlines*: the 'Elizabethan ruling fraction' was responsible for actively repressing those on the margins of society who were considered to be a threat. This was done not only by 'coercive' means such as physical punishment, seizure of property and imprisonment, but also ideologically; for example, through the demonization of masterless men, racial minorities and 'disobedient' women.[33] So Dollimore and Sinfield do not say here that ideology 'works by itself', but that it is put to work in the interests of the dominant. However, neither would it be true to say that every ideological effect is in the full control of some shadowy backroom manipulator, perhaps a fixer like Thomas Cromwell or a spymaster like Sir Francis Walsingham. To some extent ideas do take on a life of their own; in today's social media parlance they are called memes. Ideas are conceived, in some form, by an individual and received, reformulated and circulated by other individuals with whom they may gain or lose popularity, but no single person or even group of people is in full control of the effects that these ideas can have. Nevertheless, Parvini is quite right to worry about the way that ideology can sometimes seem to be utterly autonomous, and the criticism he makes here is one that has often been directed against theorists associated with anti-humanism. The expression '"beliefs, practices and institutions" just *work* by themselves' is in fact a partial quotation of a phrase used by Louis Althusser in an essay that is anti-humanist in orientation. In the next section I deal with this accusation in more detail and return to the claim that cultural materialism is sympathetic to anti-humanist writers like Althusser and Foucault.

Althusser and Foucault

As I have noted, Dollimore suggests that accusations of anti-humanism have sometimes been levelled at cultural materialism because the concept of anti-humanism itself has not been properly understood. Yet this is not the only term that has caused confusion. In their passage on *Henry V*, Dollimore and Sinfield use the term 'ideology' to refer to a way of thinking about the world that serves to justify the behaviour and power of the ruling class. This is a perfectly acceptable way of using the term, and that usage is in any case explained in the passage itself. However, Parvini's allusion to Althusser suggests that he may have understood the word in a different sense. While, as discussed in Chapter 2, cultural materialists tend to use a version of Williams's model of culture and hence speak of a dominant ideology that is put under pressure both by its own inconsistencies and by other competing residual and emergent ideologies, Althusser distinguishes between ideologies and 'ideology in general', with the latter term denoting a much 'harder' version of ideology that allows less room for contestation. In Andrew Milner's words, 'Althusser's distinctive contribution was to read Marxism as if it were a structuralism ... so that the older Western Marxist prioritization of agency and *praxis* was altogether subsumed into a general theory of structural determination.'[34] The terms of the debate are plainly laid out in this quotation: the Marxist investment in human agency, an investment that persisted in Williams's thought and, I argue, in the cultural materialist method, is devalued in Althusserianism and replaced by something like the determinism that Parvini is concerned about. Thus the relationship between the influence of Williams and Althusser upon cultural materialism is not one of sympathy but, in many cases, opposition.

This is not to say that cultural materialists have taken nothing from Althusser at all. His view of state power, for example, shares much with Dollimore and Sinfield's passage above. In 'Ideology and Ideological State Apparatuses', the piece by which literary scholars best know him, Althusser argues that state authorities maintain control by forms of coercion, which he calls Repressive State Apparatuses or RSAs, and by ideological means via Ideological State Apparatuses or ISAs, but that in practice these two are inseparable. The RSAs function, says Althusser, 'by violence', and the ISAs '*by ideology*'; none the less, the latter 'also function secondarily by repression, even if ultimately, but only ultimately, this is very attenuated and concealed, even symbolic. (There is no such thing as a purely ideological apparatus.)'[35] Thus, the notion that ideology has a material existence is important in Althusser, as it is in Williams. He argues that 'an ideology always exists in an apparatus, and its practice, or practices', before mentioning various practices that are performed for ideological reasons, such as praying and submitting to legal rules.[36] So far, so materialist. But Althusser's notion of 'ideology in general' suggests that it functions in a much more insidious manner than had previously been thought. He argues that rather than simply working to structure the way that an individual interprets their culture, for instance by circulating the xenophobic notion that all foreigners are untrustworthy, ideology structures the individual itself. Althusser begins by distinguishing between 'particular ideolo*gies*, which, whatever their form ... always express *class positions*'[37] and 'ideology in general', which is 'omnipresent, trans-historical and therefore immutable in form throughout the extent of history'.[38] At first Althusser's insistence on the universality of ideology in general makes it sound like another form of the idealism that materialists of all stripes have consistently tried to reject. However, he soon makes it clear that this conception of ideology in general is, like Freud's theory of the unconscious, to be understood as a system through which individuals as we know them come into being. The task of this system is to represent 'the imaginary relationship of individuals to their real conditions of existence'.[39] Perhaps unwisely, Althusser quickly drops the phrase 'ideology in general' and reverts simply to 'ideology', adding another level of terminological confusion to an arena that is already well stocked with misunderstandings.[40]

Nevertheless, this Althusserian version of ideology offers a compelling explanation for the relative lack of subversive behaviour throughout history; in large part, although not exclusively, it is therefore a theory of containment. Althusser's key idea was that ideology is not a set of ideas imposed upon the individual from the outside, but a process through which those very individuals are constituted. In other words, to be human was to be 'made' of and by ideology and thus to experience an imaginary relationship to real social relations. Preferring the term 'subject', which Althusser suggests disguises a subordinate relationship with a more powerful agent within an illusion of freedom, to 'individual', which suggests an idealistic self-sufficiency, he puts it like this:

> the category of the subject is constitutive of all ideology, but at the same time and immediately I add that *the category of the subject is only constitutive of all ideology insofar as all ideology has the function (which defines it) of 'constituting' concrete individuals as subjects.*[41]

Williams calls this version of ideology 'a general, monopolizing practical consciousness'.[42] Althusser, however, writing prior to the 'Ideology and Ideological State Apparatuses' essay, describes it instead as a system of representations that is 'profoundly *unconscious* ... it is above all as *structures* that [representations] impose on the vast majority of men, not via their "consciousness". They are perceived-accepted-suffered cultural objects and they act on men via a process that escapes them.'[43] This notion of an unconscious process that escapes those who go through it begins to sound a little like so-called brainwashing, and when Althusser goes on to say that subjects are recruited by, or 'interpellated' into, imaginary relationships by ideology, and that ideology functions in such a way that it 'recruits them all', his ideas start to sound very anti-humanist indeed – it is as if human beings function like mindless drones and all resistance is futile.[44]

Parvini lumps Foucault in with Althusser in his claim that cultural materialists subscribe to infallible 'systems of control', and at first glance it is easy to see why. Both theorists were acknowledged in *Political Shakespeare* as part of the 'eclectic body of work' from which cultural materialism grew and, like Althusser, Foucault has done much to contribute to the deunifying and decentring of 'Man' that Dollimore sees as a key philosophical move for the approach.[45] At the conclusion of *The Order of Things* Foucault memorably notes that 'man is an invention of a recent date. And one perhaps nearing its end'. This is not a prophecy of atomic or environmental apocalypse, but rather, in Foucault's view, a teleological inevitability given that the concept of 'Man' may well be seen out by the same 'fundamental change in the arrangements of knowledge' that brought it into being.[46] Foucault's interest in analysing the past through what he calls discourses rather than human agents has placed his work squarely in the anti-humanist category. This is because Foucault sees discourses as constitutive of subjectivity in a manner analogous to that of Althusser's ideology. In a famous example, Foucault argues that the concept of homosexuality arose not as a result of human agency but of

the appearance in nineteenth-century psychiatry, jurisprudence, and literature of a whole series of discourses on the species and subspecies of homosexuality [which] made possible a strong advance of social controls into this area of 'perversity'; but it also made possible the formation of a 'reverse' discourse: homosexuality began to speak in its own behalf, to demand that its legitimacy or 'naturality' be acknowledged.[47]

Foucault suggests here that increasingly organized methods of punishing or 'curing' what came to be known as homosexuality essentially led to its ultimate construction as an accepted sexual and cultural identity. This process is represented as purely discursive; even the demands made for homosexuality's legitimacy emanate from the discourse that speaks 'in *its* own behalf' for '*its* legitimacy'. Despite the emancipatory quality of this particular example, then, in Foucault the outlook for human agency can seem bleak. This becomes clearer when examining the role that power plays in Foucault's thought. Like Althusser's ideology, Foucault's conception of power 'gets into' the human subject and can seem to take possession of it. He writes:

the individual is not to be conceived as a sort of elementary nucleus, a primitive atom, a multiple and inert material on which power comes to fasten or against which it happens to strike, and in doing so subdues or crushes individuals. In fact, it is already one of the prime effects of power that certain bodies, certain gestures, certain discourses, certain desires, come to be identified and constituted as individuals ... The individual is an effect of power, and at the same time, or precisely to the extent to which it is that effect, it is the element of its articulation. The individual which power has constituted is at the same time its vehicle.[48]

So far away are we now from the 'irenic and mediatory ethic' of humanism that the individual in this passage has become nothing more than an effect and a vehicle. This is anti-humanism indeed. However, there are two further important points to be made: first, the so-called 'systems of control' of Althusser and Foucault are perhaps not as impregnable as they can seem; and, second, cultural materialism does not wholly accept the model of subjectivity that they offer.

Somewhat ironically, in quoting Althusser in his criticism of cultural materialism Parvini points to a way out of the anti-humanism he attributes to the approach. The phrase 'work by themselves' comes from a longer passage in which Althusser acknowledges that not every subject is helplessly interpellated into the system he has been describing:

the subjects 'work', they 'work by themselves' in the vast majority of cases, with the exception of the 'bad subjects' who on occasion provoke the intervention of one of the detachments of the (repressive) State apparatus. But the vast majority of (good) subjects work all right 'all by themselves', i.e. by ideology.[49]

As Catherine Belsey points out, Althusser identifies some of the 'bad subjects' elsewhere in the essay itself: they are the teachers whom he calls 'a kind of hero' for attempting to go against the system;[50] in Belsey's words, 'resistance warriors, solitary or in small groups, doing their hopeless best against overwhelming odds'.[51] Of course in retrospect this seems obvious: if ideology is all-pervading and irresistible, what would be the need for repressive apparatuses in the first place? In the above passage the implication is that if 'good' subjects work 'by ideology', then 'bad' subjects are bad because they have somehow avoided being interpellated into the position of 'good' subjects. Althusser doesn't say whether this is because some form of ideology has itself interpellated that subject into 'badness', but the possibility brings us closer to Williams's version of culture in which opposing ideologies compete with one another for legitimacy.[52] And on this point Soper offers a further objection. If Althusser contends that subjects 'work by themselves' because they recognize themselves in ideology, 'who', she asks, 'does the recognizing if not the subject as conceived within humanism'?[53]

The possibility of resisting ideology, or in his terms power, is also present in Foucault's model of culture. In fact, Foucault's work is full of moments of resistance that, while not easily resolved into a homogenous ethical programme, are no less significant for that. Foucault writes: 'there is a plurality of resistances … by definition they can only exist in the strategic field of power relations. But this does *not* mean that they are only a reaction or rebound … doomed to perpetual defeat.'[54] While resistance is dangerous, difficult and perhaps seemingly insignificant, it is not hopeless. Like Althusser, Foucault is interested in debunking humanism

and problematizing agency, and although his work has
many troubling implications, at base, in the words of Brent
L. Pickett, 'clearly Foucault believes that resistance can
accomplish things "on the ground" ... Foucault wants to
be engaged; he wants to further human equality through
attacking hierarchical power relations.'[55] Admittedly, both
Foucault and Althusser suppose that the 'vast majority' of
subjects are quite happy to accept the place in society that
has been carved out for them by ideology or power, and that
they do indeed 'work by themselves' as good, contributive,
law-abiding citizens. And yet, it is certainly the case that there
are more 'bad' or 'resistant' citizens than they posit, even if
that badness consists merely in breaking the speed limit once
in a while. It is true that such petty transgressions very rarely
disrupt the state's overriding aim – and this for Althusser is
why ideology exists at all – which is to 'reproduce the conditions of its production'.[56] None the less, such small moments
are not necessarily insignificant. As Dollimore suggests, if
'identity is clearly constituted by the structures of power, of
position, allegiance, and service, then any disturbance within,
or of, identity could be as dangerous to that order as to the
individual subject'.[57] In other words, if all subjects are 'within'
ideology or power, even seemingly unimportant moments of
resistance performed by one individual might threaten the
system as a whole. 'Untune that string', as Ulysses has it, 'And
hark what discord follows' (1.3.109–10).[58] Subjects who take
this refusal too far and prove genuinely troublesome to the
state are called by all sorts of names: for those who oppose
them, they might be 'terrorists' or 'subversives'; for those
who support them, they are 'freedom fighters' or perhaps
'dissidents'. As I hope will by now be clear, the latter terms
in each of these categories are significant for cultural materialism. It is to the subversive and dissident elements in culture
that cultural materialists turn their attention, and while
Althusser and Foucault's versions of ideology and power are
certainly forbidding, they are not entirely irresistible. It is to
this resistible model that cultural materialists are committed.

All this having been said, it is important not to lose sight of the role that Althusser and Foucault play in cultural materialism. The anti-essentialist, decentred human being conceived by cultural materialism is rarely completely in control of his or her own destiny. Although cultural materialists do not subscribe to the anti-humanism that Althusserianism and Foucauldianism have been read as advocating, Parvini is correct in detecting a family resemblance between some aspects of this thought and the work of Dollimore, Sinfield and others. For example, the following passage by Althusser offers a definition of political process that chimes very neatly with the approaches of Dollimore and Sinfield:

in ideology the real relation is inevitably invested in the imaginary relation, a relation that *expresses* a *will* (conservative, conformist, reformist or revolutionary), a hope or a nostalgia, rather than describing a reality ... It follows that this action can never be purely *instrumental*; the men who would use an ideology purely as a means of action, as a tool, find that they have been caught by it, implicated by it, just when they are using it and believe themselves to be absolute masters of it.[59]

Here human subjects can, then, make a willed use of ideology in the service of a specific political aim, whether or not that aim be reactionary or revolutionary. In either case, pure will is simply not enough to succeed, because ideology can indeed be a force that escapes the command of human agents. As Dollimore points out, we must remain aware of

that always present, always potentially tragic dialectic between authority and resistance whereby instability becomes a force of repression much more than a force of liberation; dominant social formations can and do reconstitute themselves around the selfsame contradictions that destabilize them, and change can also thereby become an impetus for reaction.[60]

Human deeds, especially political ones, can very quickly slip out of the control of those who enact them, and what starts off as a totally willed event often does not end that way. An emancipation can soon turn into a pogrom. As Foucault puts it, 'people know what they do; they frequently know why they do what they do; but what they don't know is what what they do does'.[61]

The works of Shakespeare give ample evidence of this principle in action. The revolutionary fervour stirred up by Brutus and Cassius by the assassination of Julius Caesar in Act 3, Scene 1 of Shakespeare's play sees them, in fear for their lives, riding 'like madmen through the gates of Rome' (3.2.262) one scene later.[62] Similarly, Macbeth's coup eventually takes on a momentum that is beyond his will:

> I am in blood
> Stepped in so far, that should I wade no more,
> Returning were as tedious as go o'er.
> Strange things I have in head, that will to hand,
> Which must be acted, ere they may be scanned.
>
> (3.4.134–8)[63]

The task given to Hamlet by the ghost of his father is to act, yet the bloody agency he is charged with is the very thing that he cannot perform. Whether he is hindered by the doubts of a rationalist, the fears of a lover or the pusillanimity of a coward, he is unable for most of the play to enact his revenge and cannot quite understand why: he remarks,

> I do not know
> Why yet I live to say this thing's to do,
> Sith I have cause, and will, and strength, and means
> To do't.
>
> (4.4.42–5)

Even without having recourse to psychoanalytical readings of the play, it is hard not to see that Hamlet is so caught up in competing ideologies – Christianity, humanism, the revenge ethic, romantic love, misogyny – that his agency is stymied. While these examples are concerned with events of national and international significance, Dollimore argues that all subversion and dissidence functions in the same way because it relies upon the fact that authority is never total:

> In a revolutionary conjuncture contradictions may contribute to the disintegration of an existing order though only (usually) through terrible suffering, victimization, and struggle. That has to be said. In a non-revolutionary conjuncture contradictions render social process the site of contest, struggle, and change. And, again, suffering, victimization, and struggle ... no matter how successful authority may be in its repressive strategies, there remains something potentially uncontrollable not only in authority's objects but in its enterprise, its rationale, and even its origin.[64]

Brutus, Macbeth and Hamlet all find themselves at moments in which historical circumstances make a revolutionary intervention possible: at the beginning of each play the contradictions in the Roman, Scottish and Danish states between different forms of tyranny – Caesar's vs the conspirators', Duncan's vs Macbeth's, Claudius's vs Fortinbras's – allow them an opportunity to step in, although as I have suggested this is not as easy as it might sound. When such grand circumstances do not exist and revolution is not on the cards, dissidence can still occur at the level of everyday society. Here we might think of various destabilizing moments in Shakespeare's comedies, such as Christopher Sly impersonating a lord in the induction to *The Taming of the Shrew*, the weaver Bottom becoming the consort of a (fairy) queen in *A Midsummer Night's Dream*, or Rosalind representing herself as both man and woman in the epilogue of *As You Like It*. What becomes of these moments is beyond the control of individuals, and they don't come out of nowhere, but they are willed. Williams was making this point as early as 1979:

however dominant a social system may be, the very
meaning of its domination involves a limitation or selection
of the activities it covers, so that by definition it cannot
exhaust all social experience, which therefore always
potentially contains space for alternative acts and alternative intentions.[65]

Or, as Sinfield puts it, 'it was the Elizabethan social structure
that produced unemployed laborers, and military leaders, but
it could not then prevent such figures *conceiving* and *enacting*
dissident practices'.[66] These moments therefore entail what
Dollimore calls 'a reactive *agency*' produced by a human subject
that has not been captured entirely by ideology or power.[67] Once
more, 'men and women make their own history, but not in
conditions of their own choosing'.

Subjective criticism

To justify the third element of his critique, that cultural
materialists practise a 'subjective' form of criticism, Parvini
points to the following passage from an essay by Sinfield on
The Merchant of Venice:

the question of principle is how readers not situated
squarely in the mainstream of Western culture today may
relate to such a powerful cultural icon as Shakespeare ...
In this essay I pursue the question as it strikes a gay man.[68]

Sinfield's direct reference to his homosexuality can still surprise
students; not, of course, because he is an out gay man, but because
he acknowledges this in the parameters of an academic essay.
Trained from the day they enter the sterile halls of academia to
abandon opinion, emotion and even the first-person pronoun
in their academic writing, students are far more scandalized
by Sinfield's prose style than who he sleeps with. This is not

merely an idiosyncrasy of Sinfield's work, but just one example of an approach that has probably never been better used than by Terence Hawkes who, for example, begins a chapter on the intersection of nature and culture in Shakespeare with the words 'I am eating fish and chips in Stratford-upon-Avon.'[69] Although for sheer transgressive pleasure it is hard to beat Dollimore's all-singing, all-dancing vision of a cross-dressing *Antony and Cleopatra* starring Shakespearean critics Peter Stallybrass or Gary Taylor as Cleopatra (Mick Jagger was too expensive) and Marjorie Garber as Antony, an essay which incidentally gives the lie to Parvini's insinuation that cultural materialism is po-faced.[70] Some students – and indeed some scholars – find it difficult to take such critical gambits seriously because they are said to 'lack objectivity', perhaps the very charge that has been used against the students themselves by lecturers keen to justify the poor mark they have given an assignment. Dollimore is not particularly happy with Parvini's use of the word 'subjective', pointing out in his review that the difference between objectivity and subjectivity is that a judgement based on the former approach can be shown to be true or false, while one based on the latter approach cannot.[71] This is fair enough, but Parvini is surely right to imply that a 'subjective' judgement is also understood to be one influenced by personal feelings or opinions. Semantics aside, several cultural materialists (and some new historicists) do draw attention to their personal experiences in their work; the question, however, is whether this tendency should be dismissed in the way that Parvini suggests. In a sense, this gets to the very heart of the practice of criticism itself. As Stanley Fish and Wolfgang Iser among others have pointed out, a reader inevitably arrives in front of a text with his or her own quirks and prejudices. If that reader is also a critic, the task is to produce not only a reading of that text that can be shown to be true or false and therefore objective, but also one that is original and thus to a certain extent influenced by personal feelings or opinions that, whether acknowledged or not, will inevitably have a political dimension. The difficulty is in judging just how far that 'certain extent' goes. Any proclamations of absolute political neutrality made by traditionalist critics can safely be met with the incredulity they deserve.

In some of their writing, Dollimore and Sinfield deliberately push that 'certain extent' to breaking point. This is what they call 'reading against the grain', a methodology that Sinfield explains at length in *Shakespeare, Authority, Sexuality*. Alluding to his essay on *The Merchant of Venice*, he runs through his argument that Antonio is in love with Bassanio, and that the play might end with the two men exiting the stage hand in hand with Portia, who must bring herself to accept her new husband's other relationship. Sinfield is well aware that this a provocative take on the play: 'my gay reading is – not exactly wrong, but, say – particular. It may be a good gay reading, but by so much as it is that, it falls outside dominant expectations. I know I am *reading against the grain*.'[72] Neither 'reading against the grain' nor reading from a 'subjective' point of view are approved of by traditional literary critics, and Parvini objects that 'the text becomes nothing more than a hook on which to hang things'[73] – but for Sinfield that is beside the point, and he makes no bones about it: 'the ultimate allegiance of the cultural materialist is not to the text as such – not to literature – but to the political project'.[74] Why should a writer such as Sinfield, who was active in the gay rights movement, be obliged to abandon his politics and his identity if he wished to discuss Shakespeare in print? To do so would be to ignore the very problematization of the 'universal' human nature that cultural materialism is predicated on. As Sinfield puts it, 'the precise tendency of Englit, especially in its current, meritocratic phase, is to detach individuals from other sub-cultural allegiances. One abandons subculture to become Man.'[75] One way to resist the 're-centring' of 'Man' encouraged by traditional criticism, then, is to cleave to groups that understand the human in ways that reject universalizing or essentializing descriptions. Once the alleged contradiction in cultural materialism between anti-humanism and individual agency has been dismissed, the only remaining objection to this kind of approach is that it demonstrates a bias that overlooks certain elements of a text. The reply of the cultural materialist is 'yes, of course it does'. As all students and all academics know, no analysis, no matter how lengthy and how detailed, will ever exhaust the works of Shakespeare (nor a good many other texts from both so-called 'low' culture and 'high'). Surely among the many billions upon billions of words written about Shakespeare, there is room for a criticism that doesn't pretend to put politics to one side, doesn't pretend to take an 'objective' viewpoint on the work, and instead confesses what it is up to loudly and clearly?

As the criticisms of 'Parvini and others like him' shows, it is still not easy, even thirty years after the publication of *Political Shakespeare*, for this aspect of cultural materialism to be accepted. While it is probably fair to say that the rejection of conservative grand narratives, the nuancing of the concept of historical context and the liberal use of theory have largely become accepted in the academy, the political commitment that is so significant in cultural materialism has had a tougher reception. As Sinfield wrote in 2006, 'a project for cultural materialism, still, is to acknowledge that its readings may be partial, novel and strenuously pursued (as indeed, everyone else's may be) without accepting that this must entail an abdication of authority'.[76] During the past decade, in a Shakespeare studies that has been proclaimed 'post-theory', that has seen a rehabilitation of character as a locus of analysis as well as turns to humanism, spirituality, antiquarianism and neurology, that task is more difficult than ever. Yet I wonder whether Sinfield's concerns about academic authority still matter. Whatever is going on inside the walls of academia, there are signs that the politically inflected, anti-essentialist, against-the-grain readings of the cultural materialists are being taken up by the culture at large. In May 2016, BBC One aired a version of *A Midsummer Night's Dream*, adapted by *Queer as Folk* and *Doctor Who* writer Russell T. Davies, in which Puck's love potion causes Demetrius to become temporarily infatuated with Lysander as well as Helena and, more radically, a tyrannical Theseus dies leaving Hippolyta to live happily ever after with her lover Titania. As a partial, novel and strenuously pursued reading of the play this is very much in the spirit of Dollimore and Sinfield, who could scarcely have done better themselves.

Another example takes place entirely outside of the realms of the dramatic, the scholarly, or the literary. In February 2015, Tin Man Games released a multiplatform computer 'gamebook adventure' called *To Be or Not to Be* that allows players to experience *Hamlet* from the point of view of some of its characters.[77] Written by 'Ryan North, William Shakespeare and You', *To Be or Not to Be* is a text-based game that asks users to decide what either Ophelia ('an awesome lady in her late 20s, with a calm, competent, and resourceful demeanour'), Hamlet ('an emo teen in his early 30s') or Hamlet, Sr. ('Spoiler alert: you get ghost powers and then must INVESTIGATE YOUR OWN MURDER') should do in situations that are familiar from Shakespeare's play. The plot decisions that Shakespeare made are marked on the screen with a skull, and there are usually several other paths to choose instead. So while it is perfectly possible for the player to decide to ignore the precedent that Shakespeare set, the range of alternatives they have is limited. We might say that players can make their own story, but not in conditions entirely of their own choosing. If they decide to ignore Shakespeare's example, players can find themselves fighting skeletons or becoming ninjas. But things are not straightforward even if players do decide to follow the plot as Shakespeare set it down. For instance, at the end of what, in the play, would be Act 1 Scene 2, the player embodying Hamlet can choose to either play solitaire until it is late enough for the ghost to appear, or follow Shakespeare's lead and 'Be Ophelia for a while'. Ophelia, who is studying physics at university and in her spare time working on introducing central heating to Elsinore, is, as in Shakespeare, given some brotherly advice by Laertes: 'If you sleep with Hamlet you're a slut,' he says. If the player-as-Ophelia then does as Shakespeare's Ophelia did and decides to let Laertes continue his speech, the interface responds with a puzzled 'O-okay?' The more the player continues to make Shakespearean choices in this scene, the more incredulous the interface becomes, and when Polonius forbids Ophelia from seeing Hamlet again the last straw seems to have been reached. After this point Ophelia's available responses to her father are 'Slap him across his face and tell him you're not dumb and you can recognize sincere emotion in a sexual partner when you see it,' or the Shakespearean

> Tell him – you'll obey? And then call him your lord. And … follow him meekly out of the room? Agree with everything he and Laertes have said, because all that stuff I wrote earlier about you being an independent woman in charge of her own destiny sounds PRETTY DUMB ACTUALLY, and you'd better do whatever someone else tells you to, because anyone other than you probably knows better about your own life than you do, right? Look, I am now trying to think of the dumbest thing you can do. Please, I beg you, do not choose this option.[78]

This is a playful, revisionist re-reading of Hamlet that actively draws attention to the historical difference that intervenes between our era and Shakespeare's, that allows agency within some prescribed limits and that is feminist in orientation. It may not have the same kind of authority that attaches itself to the latest pronouncements of eminent Shakespeareans, but it doesn't need it. Like Davies's *A Midsummer Night's Dream*, this is a cultural artefact that has pleasure on its side. As Sinfield points out, 'pleasure in Shakespeare is a complex phenomenon, and it may not be altogether incompatible with a critical attitude to ideology in the plays'.[79] That critical attitude is called cultural materialism.

4

Past vs Present: Cultural Materialism and Contemporary Politics

Mirrors

Rousing the audience to a state of excitement that matches his own, the Chorus of Shakespeare's *King Henry V* proclaims that, at the prospect of war with France,

> Now all the youth of England are on fire,
> And silken dalliance in the wardrobe lies.
> …
> They sell the pasture now to buy the horse,
> Following the mirror of all Christian kings.
>
> $(2.0.1–2, 5–6)^1$

Although that final phrase is unfamiliar to modern ears, it is clear from the context that by calling Henry a 'mirror' the Chorus is paying him a compliment. In fact, the word is a now archaic synonym for 'paragon', and its use in a play like *Henry V* is appropriate since it recalls a genre of books known as 'mirrors for princes'. These books advised rulers on how to conduct themselves effectively, and since most of the examples they gave were of benevolent role models (Machiavelli's *The Prince* being a notable exception) the meaning of 'mirror' expanded to refer not only to written examples but also lived exemplars. But of course the word also means a piece of glass or other polished surface in which a reflection can be seen, and thus something that imitates another thing. In *King Richard III*, for example, the Duchess of York bemoans the loss of her sons Edward and Clarence by comparing them to their father, who is also dead: 'But now two mirrors of his princely semblance / Are cracked in pieces by malignant death' (2.2.51–2).[2] In Shakespeare, then, a mirror can be a perfect example worthy of emulation or an accurate reflection of something else. A similar duality has been present in Shakespeare criticism from the very beginning. One of the earliest pieces of such criticism, Ben Jonson's famous commendatory poem 'To the memory of my beloved', included in the 1623 First Folio of Shakespeare's plays, praises Shakespeare in a tone reminiscent of the Chorus from *Henry V*. Jonson celebrates Shakespeare's originality saying, among other things, 'He was not of an age, but for all time' and calling him 'star of poets'.[3] Conversely, in prefatory material for the 1632 Second Folio, a poem by a writer identified as I.M.S. praises Shakespeare for his ability to recreate the past in a convincing and engaging manner:

> A mind reflecting ages past, whose clear
> And equal surface can make things appear
> Distant a thousand years, and represent
> Them in their lively colours' just extent.[4]

Two ways of understanding Shakespeare's dramatic legacy are offered in these contrasting lines. Either his skill is a form of unfettered creativity not bound to any era, or it is, while no less creative, an art of reflection that depends for its success on what already exists, be it the past invoked by I.M.S. or Shakespeare's own era, now become the 'ages past' that twenty-first-century readers must deal with whenever they encounter his work.

These two positions – that Shakespeare reflects his historical moment or transcends it – are echoed in every critical debate about the extent to which history informs literature. As I argued in the last chapter, one of the distinctive characteristics of the cultural materialist position is that it advocates an active role for Shakespeare: his works are not just reflective but in fact constitute a series of interventions into culture, albeit to varying extents and with varying effects. As Jonathan Dollimore puts it, 'literature was a practice which intervened in contemporary history in the very act of representing it'.[5] And as Catherine Belsey notes, we should remember that even in their own era, 'fictional texts do not necessarily mirror the practices prevalent in a social body, but they are a rich repository of the meanings its members understand and contest'.[6] These kinds of critical debates are necessary and often fruitful; however, of equal interest are those that relate to perhaps the most commonly understood meaning of the word 'mirror', which has so far been neglected: the mirror as something that reflects back the self that looks into it. Approaching literature from this perspective can have different effects depending on the temporal relationship between the work that is 'looked into', and the person doing the looking. The more proximate an artefact and its audience are in time, the more provocative the 'text as mirror' idea can be. One of the best examples of this is a performance of Shakespeare's *King Richard II* that was staged in February 1601/2 at the request of the Earl of Essex. Formerly one of Elizabeth I's court favourites, Essex's relationship with the queen had soured, and after a disastrous military campaign in Ireland in 1599 he endured eleven months of house arrest on his return. Upon regaining his freedom Essex decided to march to the palace with as many supporters as he could muster and demand that the queen offer him a position of influence, perhaps even the crown itself. To stir up support, he paid the Lord Chamberlain's Men, Shakespeare's company of players, to perform a play about Richard II, which was almost certainly Shakespeare's.[7] While opinions about Essex's motivations differ, it seems likely that the play's deposition scene, in which Richard agrees to relinquish the crown to his cousin Henry Bolingbroke, was thought by Essex to have been a useful reminder to the play's spectators that monarchs can be, and have been, removed from power.[8] Essex's coup did not attract the support it needed, but Elizabeth seemed to recognize the power of *Richard II* since she ordered the removal of the deposition scene from all subsequent printings of the play, and is reported to have said 'I am Richard II. Know ye not that?'[9] Reactions to plays usually become less fraught as the date of the composition of a text moves further and further away from the date of its reception, and historically distant audiences begin to see through a glass not necessarily darkly, but differently. Nevertheless, in the right context and with the right emphasis, modern productions of Shakespeare can cause remarkable reactions among their audiences. For example, in 1995 Gregory Doran staged a production of *Titus Andronicus* in South Africa where the ruling Romans of the play were performed as Afrikaners and the Goths as a multi-racial revolutionary guerrilla force. By tapping into racial tensions in a recently post-Apartheid South Africa in this way, Doran was able to engender great sympathy in his audiences for the black character of Aaron, who is received negatively by most audiences due to his involvement in the play in rape, mutilation and murder.[10]

In productions like these it is easy to see Shakespeare as a means of reflecting contemporary culture back upon itself, particularly in its most painful, awkward or disputed aspects. In *Richard II* Elizabeth saw a threat to her power; in *Titus Andronicus*, black South Africans saw a celebration of theirs. Writing about Shakespeare in 1939, Esther Cloudman Dunn put it like this:

Into his book, each age has peered, as into a mirror, to see its own face. The images in that mirror fade and are replaced as decades go by. But the mirror is not discarded. There is a strange compulsion to look into it, to scrutinise this

Shakespeare, no matter how cramped and dated the era may be. He responds by showing only so much of himself as is comely in the eyes of the particular world which reads him.[11]

This is an early version of an approach to Shakespeare later adopted by cultural materialists and perhaps best expressed – certainly most pithily – by Terence Hawkes: 'Shakespeare doesn't mean: *we* mean *by* Shakespeare.'[12] Hawkes's formulation improves on Dunn's by replacing the mysterious agency of a mirror-Shakespeare with, first, the active deployment of Shakespeare for ideological purposes by those with authority in the academic, dramatic and political spheres, and, second, a potential contestation of those meanings by everyone else; Hawkes says of the plays 'we *use* them in order to generate meaning'.[13] This is an immensely valuable insight; however, if applied unwisely it can serve to erase the multiple material contexts within which a text was produced. Michael Bristol cautions:

Hawkes is certainly right to argue that the interpretation of a literary work is never a simple matter of passive submission to an author's intention. The activity of inter-pretation is always socially interested. However, it does not follow from these insights that literary works are themselves vacuous.[14]

For some critics, close reading is enough to offset this threatened vacuity; for cultural materialists, as we have seen, Hawkes's notion of using Shakespeare to generate meaning will only be effective if it combines 'historical context, theoretical method, political commitment and textual analysis'.[15]

Yet if, as discussed in the previous chapter, cultural materialists argue that certain configurations of historical circumstances can reveal ideological faultlines in which it becomes possible for social change to occur, as Dunn hints it follows that those same cultural shifts can sometimes bring our present into meaningful conversation with elements of *relevance highlights certain aspects* [handwritten annotation]

Shakespeare's plays that might at other moments in time have remained irrelevant, and thus hidden. Such historical movements can be profound and traumatic, and can open up profound, traumatic readings of Shakespeare. For example, in the twenty-first century no one can engage with *The Merchant of Venice* without reading it in the context of the Holocaust. While anti-Semitism was certainly rife prior to, during and after Shakespeare's era, the enormity of that twentieth-century event has forever refocused interpretations of the play.[16] Just as importantly, *The Merchant of Venice* might itself prompt a reader to reassess some aspects of his or her own cultural moment. This is a significant aspect of the cultural materialist method: Alan Sinfield calls it 'an attentiveness to historically located formations' and celebrates the possibility that such 'historical engagement might discompose the present'.[17] But cultural materialism does not suggest that the only thing we see in the mirror held up by Shakespeare is ourselves. To press the metaphor a little further, as is the case when we look into any mirror we also see something else: the distortions that that mirror introduces – tiny splatters of toothpaste and face cream, or even just the inevitable reversal of the reflected image, are also perceived by the viewer, reminding them that what they see is not a completely accurate version of themselves. By adopting the 'partial' reading tactic discussed in the last chapter, a reader who identifies *with* something in Shakespeare is not identifying *themselves*, but seeing instead the difference between, on the one hand, the way that they recognize themselves in their own cultural moment, and, on the other, unfamiliar echoes of that recognition in Shakespeare. In other words, cultural materialism pays attention to meanings that become visible in the gap introduced by historical difference, the difference between perceptions of the Shakespearean past and the contemporary present. For Dollimore, historical engagement not only discomposes the present but, crucially, also reveals that we have never seen that present very clearly in the first place. He thus advocates an approach that would entail a greater effort of historical understanding: one adequate to comprehend, challenge, and maybe even change those recalcitrant, destructive human realities which we inherit and therefore live and perpetuate so stubbornly. An effort of understanding which knows that we always risk misrecognizing the realities we live, and the struggles they imply, and that going back into the past via intellectual history is one way of reducing that risk.[18]

This notion of exposing misrecognition depends upon historicizing Althusser's definition of ideology as 'the imaginary relationship of individuals to their real conditions of existence', and while cultural materialists do not pretend that such an approach is easy they do consider it worth attempting.[19]

Cultural materialism's bifocal interest in the past and the present distinguishes it from more straightforward historicist readings of Shakespeare and from the critical approach known as presentism. The former attitude is summed up by David Scott Kastan, who wants to save Shakespeare from what he calls the 'narcissism' of cultural materialism and new historicism by ensuring that when scholars interpret Shakespeare 'what we hear are his concerns rather than projections of our own'.[20] In advocating a presentist approach, Hugh Grady and Terence Hawkes poke fun at Kastan's position by referring to presentism as a supposed 'sinister enemy' of Shakespeare and invoking the 'nightmare situation' in which 'contact with the actualities and particular contingencies of the past is felt to have been contaminated by the critic's own "situatedness" in the present'.[21] They point out, as do cultural materialists, that no such antiseptic contact with the past will ever be possible, and that temporal situatedness should therefore be embraced. However, they go on to claim that the tendency to assess Shakespeare's plays alongside other non-literary documents 'has been singularly reductive. In particular it has obscured how the works function for us in the present'.[22] Thus Grady and Hawkes break with the cultural materialist impulse to use such contemporaneous material to pry open the gap introduced by historical difference a little further than might otherwise be possible.[23] Looking back at the subversion/containment debate, Evelyn Gajowski sharpens this point when she laments the way that 'eventually, historicists came to represent as subversive in early modern England that which was drained of any subversive power in the present'.[24] Grady, Hawkes and Gajowski are of course correct to warn of the drift towards political quietism that can occur in some historicist criticism; after all, that was one of the tendencies against which cultural materialism was formulated. But as Lucy Munro has recently argued, if the case against historicism *per se* is overstated, presentist 'critics run the risk both of caricaturing "historicism" as a reactionary and a-theoretical monolith, and of subsuming all criticism of which they approve into an equally undifferentiated "presentism"'.[25] It would be grossly unfair if cultural materialism were to fall foul of this approach, either by misrepresentation or by neglect. Its characteristically utopian position in this debate is, in Sinfield's phrase, 'wanting the best of both worlds', and while historicism privileges the past and presentism the present, cultural materialism attempts to keep the two in dialogue by looking, so to speak, through both sides of the mirror.[26]

In the rest of this chapter, I will look more closely at some of these interventions in order to show how they use an analysis of the Shakespearean past in order to intervene politically in the present. One of the striking things about cultural materialism is the attention it pays to the practice of teaching Shakespeare, and it is with this topic that I begin. I then move on to examine the approach's engagement with issues of race and nationality, before turning finally to sexuality and gender. What follows is very far from exhaustive, but does offer a flavour of the work that has been done under a cultural materialist aegis.

Classroom

As befits a methodology concerned with political intervention, cultural materialism had some practical beginnings. Its intellectual origins, together with those of many allied leftist critical approaches to literature, can be traced to the theoretical revolution of the late 1970s and what John Drakakis calls 'a radical re-mapping of an entire intellectual terrain', but key ideas really began to coalesce around a series of conferences and an accompanying journal, both called 'Literature Teaching Politics [LTP]'.[27] LTP was, in Helen Taylor's words, 'a network of radical work in English studies' that comprised 'regional groups, six journals [issues], seven conferences and one set of conference papers' running from 1979 until 1987.[28] It is no coincidence that LTP was formed in the same year that Margaret Thatcher became Prime Minister; as Martin Blocksidge points out, 'Shakespeare criticism in the 1980s was not only radical in method, but, politically, explicitly oppositional at a time when the Conservative government was taking a hostile stance towards universities, and by extension, to intellectuals generally.'[29] As I discussed in Chapter 1, one way in which that anti-intellectualism manifested itself was through the pronouncements of Conservative politicians such as Nigel Lawson about the timeless reactionary values that Shakespeare supposedly endorsed. But Thatcherite attacks on university culture went beyond rhetoric to include the introduction of competition into Higher Education via the compilation of league tables, the reform of the university funding mechanism and hence the closure of 'unprofitable' departments, and the phasing out of student maintenance grants in favour of loans.[30] Members of LTP were determined to combat such attitudes and, as the name of the network suggests, the classroom was one of its key battlegrounds. Dollimore and Sinfield have testified to the way that LTP empowered them to teach Shakespeare politically:

> Before LTP, teachers were political in the union, feminist groups or whatever; but to politicise your teaching, for many of us, seemed somehow improper ... LTP afforded both the language and the confidence to 'come out' specifically in teaching as a socialist/feminist/gay/unilateralist.[31]

Contributors to *LTP*, the journal, included Dollimore and Sinfield as well as now celebrated scholars such as Simon Barker, Catherine Belsey, Alison Light, Kiernan Ryan, Peter Stallybrass, Chris Weedon and others, so it is clear that the discipline of English has to a certain extent been able to accept the radical politics it was struggling against in the early 1980s. Thirty-five years or so later, teaching English politically can still feel improper at times – and student comments such as 'too much politics!' do occasionally appear on module evaluation forms – but that only demonstrates how significant the original task of politicizing the subject was.[32] Indeed, Isobel Armstrong calls it 'profoundly surprising, given the usual quietism of British academic critical discourse'.[33] The editorial team for *LTP*'s first issue offers a manifesto that has much in common with Dollimore and Sinfield's descriptions of cultural materialism:

> The aim of LTP is to analyse the plurality of relations between literature, teaching and politics, as a basis for change. Some of the main concerns of LTP have been the politics of established modes of textual analysis, cultural production and teaching. These concerns are directed towards the construction of new critical and teaching practices which take account of developments in Marxism and feminism.[34]

Although, as I discuss later in this chapter, the role of feminism has been contested, and Dollimore himself has recently admitted 'I don't think I've been Marxist enough', the emphasis in the passage on political intervention, on exposing the politics of traditional modes of 'doing English', and on developing new theoretically informed approaches to criticism are very much aligned with the cultural materialist agenda.[35] But perhaps the most striking thing about this passage, and about the content of *LTP* itself, is the emphasis placed on the actual practice of teaching English. And not just university teaching: the first article in the first issue of *LTP*, by Holly Goulden and John Hartley, offers a detailed Marxist critique of the way that English is taught and examined at British secondary schools and sixth-form colleges.[36]

In a piece first published in *LTP* and then revised for *Faultlines*, Sinfield offers practical advice for educators struggling to find ways of teaching reactionary but canonical texts to students. The problem with such texts, Sinfield points out, is that while the dominant fraction of society is usually represented in a positive manner,

> certain groups are denied any existence at all, or granted it only on condition that they appear bad or, lately, sick. Generally this is true of lower-class people discontented with their lot, especially if they try to do anything about it, certainly if they try to organise; it is true of many possibilities for women; and, of course, of gay men and lesbians.[37]

Sinfield suggests four ways of dealing with this problem: if a teacher is able to select their own syllabus they may simply exclude the offending text; they can 'strenuously interpret' it in order to emphasize its suppressed progressive qualities; or they may argue that the offensive content was not really the 'truth' of the text but rather a mere formal effect. The fourth and most useful approach, Sinfield suggests, is to return the text to its historical contexts, thus allowing it to be seen as 'a project devised within a certain set of practices ... producing a version of reality which is promulgated as meaningful and persuasive at a certain historical conjuncture'. Once this is done, 'the values stated or implied in the text are no longer an embarrassment, for we need not expect to endorse them'.[38] Of course, as Charles H. Frey observes, some students may be shocked to discover that the Shakespeare venerated by their culture espouses such values at all. Nevertheless, Frey argues, 'it is an absolutely primary function of high school and college education – is it not? – to enhance the student's willingness and ability to reconsider received ideologies, of whatever persuasion'.[39]

Work in this vein was an important feature of *Political Shakespeare*, the second section of which included two essays by Sinfield on Shakespeare and education. The first of these takes a similar approach to Goulden and Hartley in that it reveals the idealist assumptions inherent in the teaching of Shakespeare at school level. Sinfield's thesis is broadly Althusserian in the terms set out in the previous chapter: the education system is an ISA charged with the task of reproducing the conditions of its production, but there is an 'element of play in the system [that] indicates the scope for radical intervention'.[40] Sinfield pays particular attention to the phrasing of examination questions set for sixteen- and eighteen-year-olds in 1983, and argues that through these the dominant ideology sustains itself in two (by now familiar) ways: by projecting 'local conditions on to the eternal' and constructing 'individual subjectivity as a given which is undetermined and unconstituted and hence a ground of meaning and coherence'.[41] But some potential for resistance, or at least appropriation, can be found when students are invited to reconstruct Shakespeare in their own terms; for example, an exam question on *As You Like It* asked sixteen-year-old pupils to 'Write an editorial for the *Arden Gazette* on the recent outbreak of marriage in the district.' Such invitations match Sinfield's interest in partial, against-the-grain readings that, as he puts it here, undermine 'the procedures of Literature'.[42] In an essay written nine years after the first and included in the second edition of *Political Shakespeare*, Sinfield revisits the topic in the light of the then new General Certificate of Secondary Education (GCSE) course introduced to assess fourteen- to sixteen-year-olds. He concludes that the new examinations are predicated upon the same assumptions

as before, but that they offer even less scope for independence
of thought or the exercise of intelligence: 'the tests aspire to
produce a smothering of creativity, of imaginative potential'.[43]
Graham Holderness and Marcus Nevitt substantiate this point
in their analysis of the first mandatory Shakespeare examination paper of June 1993, a paper that was, in the event,
boycotted by 600,000 fourteen-year-old students.[44] Despite
the boycott, the then Prime Minister John Major persisted
with the reforms and sought to score points with the right
wing of his party by picking a battle with academics who
objected to them.[45] Again, for Sinfield hope lies in students'
personal rewritings, and thus intelligent reassessments, of
Shakespeare. He offers a striking example of this in action
when he shows how a version of *Macbeth* rewritten by a
ten-year-old child can prompt questions about the role played
by collective democratic action in challenging state power and
religious superstition.[46]

Consideration of this topic continues in *The Shakespeare
Myth*, which contains an essay by David Hornbrook and
two interviews with theatre practitioners on the topic of
Shakespearean drama in education. The interviews, with
John Hodgson, Head of Drama at Bretton Hall College, and
Michael Croft, Director of the National Youth Theatre, reveal
the materialist and idealist alternatives in this debate. For
Hodgson, although literary theory is 'stifling', it is important
nevertheless that student actors 'try to experience life as it was
then'.[47] Involvement in Shakespearean drama can ultimately
help students understand 'how, when and why' it might
be appropriate to work towards political change in the
present day.[48] Croft, however, while sceptical of Shakespeare's
universal status, is keen to hold on to 'the intention of the
text' and aims to inculcate a lifelong taste for Shakespeare in
young people, which he suggests would best be achieved by
abolishing all examinations and teaching the arts 'for pleasure
only'.[49] For Croft, a young person need only be exposed to
the language of the plays for 'the magic of Shakespeare' to
do its work.[50] Like Sinfield, Hornbrook rejects the idealist

perspective espoused by Croft, and argues that Shakespeare's plays must be understood as something other than means by which a supposed universal human essence can be revealed. However, in addressing the popular classroom strategy of making Shakespeare 'relevant' by asking students to put the plays into terms that they can more easily understand, Hornbrook also offers a warning. If relevance is all, and 'Macbeth's ambitions for the crown of Scotland may be likened to a boy's desire to be captain of the football team, urged on perhaps by a sister or girlfriend', then Shakespeare's work may as well be replaced by 'material with less literary encumbrance'.[51] The danger inherent in Sinfield's valorization of partial readings produced in the classroom, then, is that unless such readings are adequately historicized, they might come to be understood as the erasure, not the revelation of historical difference. The task of historicization is a lot to ask of teachers, who are already overworked and demoralized by a system that places far more value on league tables than it does on learning. Nevertheless, for Hornbrook the alternative is 'the perpetuation of powerlessness'.[52]

Ann Thompson, also broadly in sympathy with the cultural materialist project, offers a revealing example of how the approach can run into problems at university level, despite the best intentions of academics. After sketching out a syllabus organized on historicist principles, she notes that most English lecturers are not '"real" historians and that we cannot provide expert teaching in this area ... always, we face the problem of having too much material to squeeze into the finite parameters of our courses'.[53] Thompson also encountered 'considerable resistance' to the politicization of Shakespeare from students 'who actually prefer to distance the text from the sort of debate that would oblige us to confront directly the continuing inequalities of the British class system'.[54] These issues seem to me intractable at all levels, at least so long as a set syllabus must be covered. It is perhaps only when a student is allowed the freedom to develop a dissertation-length study that the balancing of text, context and political present can come to fruition. While UK universities are, at the time of writing, mercifully exempt from government interference in curricula, this state of affairs is threatened by the proposed 'Teaching Excellence Framework', a set of information-gathering mechanisms designed to evaluate teaching. This legislation is still under discussion, but if approved the TEF may allow the government to take an aggressive role in assessing what it defines as 'teaching quality' and potentially in prescribing the content of lectures, seminars and assessments.

At school level, of course, such oversight is here to stay, and Sarah Olive confirms that little has changed in the last twenty years to alter the Conservative-led reforms of the 1990s. She argues that during their period of office from 1997 to 2010, Labour made 'minimal changes to policy concerning Shakespeare in the National Curriculum',[55] and that 'the adoption of a more radically left-wing position of treating all culture, and all knowledges, as equal through abolishing existing hierarchies within the curriculum was incontrovertibly eschewed'.[56] Under the regime of the Conservative–Liberal Democrat coalition (2010–15), the Secretary of State for Education, Michael Gove, advocated a traditionalist curriculum even more antiquated than that of the Thatcher government and adopted an 'unashamedly conservative definition of inclusivity as assimilation into great English (at a pinch, British) authors'.[57] In an echo of Major's quarrel with those opposed to GCSE reforms, Gove dismissed 100 academics who publicly objected to his policies as 'bad academia' and claimed that their views were straightforward 'prejudice'.[58] Gove's disdain for those with knowledge and experience of education is at least consistent, given that Matt White, assistant director of the Department for Education's national curriculum review, admitted that some elements of the new curriculum had been drawn up without any consultation from experts whatsoever.[59] Moreover, by accusing education professionals of prejudice, Gove uses against his opponents the very language of inclusivity that his own curriculum reforms reject. When it is those with demonstrable expertise who are 'prejudiced' and 'bad', and those who make decisions without consultation fair and balanced, we are truly in the depths of ideology.[60] This is an excellent illustration of the way that, in Dollimore's terms, 'dominant social formations can and do reconstitute themselves around the selfsame contradictions that destabilize them, and change can also thereby become an impetus for reaction'.[61]

Race and nation

Since one of the key concerns of cultural materialism is the dynamic between dominant and marginal cultures, it is no surprise that the approach has often been deployed to consider questions of race and nationality. Shakespeare's *The Tempest*, with its representation of a powerful European magus enacting his will upon two natives of a mysterious island, has naturally been a key proving-ground for cultural materialists. The play is all the more open to such a methodology since its origins can in part be traced to two contemporaneous 'non-literary' texts: a 1609 account of the wreck of an English ship off the coast of Bermuda, and Michel de Montaigne's essay 'Of the Caniballes'.[62] In 2016 it is difficult to see how any analysis could fail to acknowledge the issues of racial prejudice and colonial power present in *The Tempest*, but prior to the 1950s such readings were rare.[63] When in 'Invisible Bullets' Stephen Greenblatt pursued his case about subversion and containment – a case built upon an encounter between English colonists and Native Americans – with reference to the Henriad instead of *The Tempest*, the play was briefly ceded to cultural materialism, and two complementary essays mapped out the territory.[64] In a piece for *Political Shakespeare*, Paul Brown shows how power attempts to legitimate itself through the production of its own potential subversion, but that that subversion ensures the relationship between the colonizer and the colonized is one of perpetual struggle. Brown offers as a key example the moment in Act 4 of the play when Prospero, seemingly in command of everything seen and heard by the characters onstage and the audience offstage, suddenly interrupts the elaborate wedding masque he has arranged and exclaims:

> I had forgot that foul conspiracy
> Of the beast Caliban and his confederates
> Against my life.
>
> (4.1.139–41)[65]

Brown argues that Prospero is aware that Caliban's proposed coup is laughable, and yet,

> It is *he* who largely produces the ineffectual challenge as a dire threat. This is to say, the colonialist narrative requires and produces the other – an other which continually destabilises and disperses the narrative's moment of conviction. The threat must be present to validate colonialist discourse; yet if present it cannot but impel the narrative to further action.[66]

Brown's point is that the logic of colonialism is imperilled by the logic of narrative, since, as formulated, the colonialist struggle is never-ending, and all texts are necessarily finite. Brown suggests that *The Tempest* can only end if Prospero-as-colonist gives up his domination of the play and colonialism is therefore displaced as its central concern. Thus it is Gonzalo, not Prospero, who announces the resolution of the play when he articulates a desire to memorialize its strange events, to 'set it down / With gold on lasting pillars' (5.1.207–8), while Prospero, no longer in control of all that he has arranged, 'is in danger of becoming the other to the narrative declaration of his own project'.[67] In other words, the colonial project is a perpetual and anxious one that legitimates itself by producing, resisting and then reproducing its subversion; it is only in narrative that that subversion can be contained, albeit imperfectly. On this reading, the value of *The Tempest* is as 'a limit text in which the characteristic operations of colonialist discourse may be discerned'.[68]

Francis Barker and Peter Hulme's essay in *Alternative Shakespeares* concurs with Brown's in its desire to recognize *The Tempest* as 'a play imbricated within the discourse of colonialism', and it also sees Prospero's reaction to Caliban's 'plot' as a significant moment for understanding the role of colonialism in the play.[69] However, their piece stands as a more effective political intervention than Brown's due to the attention it pays to a series of 'disavowals'. The first is Prospero's disavowal of Caliban's prior claim to the island and construction of him as 'a born devil, on whose nature / Nurture can never stick' (4.1.188–9), a disavowal that Barker and Hulme suggest 'is itself performative of the discourse of colonialism, since this particular reticulation of denial of dispossession with retrospective justification for it, is the characteristic trope by which European colonial regimes articulated their authority'.[70] This legitimation of superiority is re-emphasized by Prospero when he foils Caliban's rebellion, and although that moment is stage-managed, Prospero's 'version of history remains *authoritative*'.[71] Unlike Brown, for Barker and Hulme the anxiety surrounding the colonial project is represented not through the displacement of Prospero, but the displacement, throughout the play, of the rebellion plot into a comic mode, an action they see as a disavowal of the disquieting implications of colonialism. The final disavowal is that of 'European and North American critics, who have tended to listen exclusively to Prospero's voice', thus ignoring both Caliban and the way that the play reveals the complexity of the encounter between Europe and the New World.[72]

Ania Loomba, one of the most significant critics to analyse the relationship between Shakespeare and colonialism through a cultural materialist lens, develops this point by noting that since the 1950s *The Tempest* has acted for Caribbean intellectuals as 'a powerful cultural symbol to be seized and used for their own ends'.[73] Although Loomba suggests that not all political

uses of *The Tempest* necessarily constitute a close engagement
with the play itself, its appropriation on behalf of struggles
against colonialism nevertheless represents one of the central
elements of cultural materialist practice in action. By making
a text that had seemed to endorse colonial authority speak
otherwise, writers like the Barbadian George Lamming – who
in *The Pleasures of Exile* (1960) uses Caliban as a figurehead
for Caribbean postcolonial literature – and Aimé Césaire from
Martinique – whose 1969 play *Une Tempête* positions Caliban
as a black slave and Prospero as his white master – are doing
exactly what Dollimore and Sinfield advocate: producing
readings of *The Tempest* that were, for their time, partial and
against-the-grain, and using those readings to make serious
political interventions.[74] Little wonder that Loomba suggests
that such writers were 'far ahead of the Shakespearian scholarship of their day'.[75] That contrast is particularly pronounced
when Loomba refers to a now notorious critical introduction
to *The Tempest* penned by Frank Kermode for the 1954 Arden
edition of the play. In considering the conditions of the play's
reproduction in the British theatre, Loomba notes that it was
not until 1934 that Caliban was represented onstage as black,
earlier depictions having shown him in a variety of animalistic,
piscine or 'wild man' guises. None the less, Loomba argues
that whatever the character actually looked like, 'Caliban's
political colour [w]as clearly *black*'.[76] She cites a passage from
Kermode's introduction to support this:

> If Aristotle was right in arguing that 'men … who are as
> much inferior to others as the body is to the soul … are
> slaves by nature, and it is advantageous for them to be
> always under government' … then the black and mutilated
> cannibal must be the natural slave of the European
> gentleman and, *a fortiori*, the salvage [*sic*] and deformed
> Caliban of the learned Prospero.[77]

Scott Wilson has argued that this passage is an ideological effect
of a critical practice, the practice, that is, of a traditionalist

criticism that 'relies, as its most basic assumption, on the notion of the superiority of the sophisticated European subject or individual who embodies, in an ideal form, the economic, colonial power of Western civilization'.[78] For Wilson, then, neither Kermode himself nor 1950s attitudes in general are to blame for statements like this; rather, it is literary criticism that uses context merely to 'set off the literary gem' that generates them.[79] While I think Wilson is a little too keen to exonerate Kermode, his account of traditional criticism is spot on: this is yet another example of the self-satisfied, Eurocentric, idealist critical attitude that cultural materialism sought to expose and replace. Loomba is less forgiving than Wilson: for her, the passage by Kermode displays 'obvious bias' that discounts any suggestion of the introduction's 'political innocence'.[80]

Despite the clear importance of *The Tempest* for analyses of Shakespeare and colonialism, Loomba cautions that 'the Caliban–Prospero relationship needs always to be set against other representations, rather than taken as symbolizing the entire encounter between Europe and its "others"'.[81] That encounter was also dramatized, for instance, in *Antony and Cleopatra* and *Othello*. One important distinction Loomba draws between *The Tempest* and these plays is that while the former engages with the New World, the latter deal with European relations with the East. As she points out, 'if Caliban is a means of discussing the contours of the colonization of the Americas, [Cleopatra and Othello] allow us to open up the question of Europe's interaction with the "old world"'.[82] Thus while Caliban is represented as savage, Cleopatra is both divine – she is described by Enobarbus as 'O'erpicturing that Venus where we see / The fancy outwork nature' (2.2.210–11) – and gloriously human, 'a lass unparalleled' in Charmian's affectionate tribute (5.2.315).[83] Othello is initially both charismatically well-spoken, having wooed Desdemona with tales of his adventures, and awkwardly formal in some of his responses, especially in these stilted remarks to the senators:

> I do agnize
> A natural and prompt alacrity
> I find in hardness, and do undertake
> This present war against the Ottomites.
>
> $(1.3.232-5)$[84]

Once Iago has finished poisoning him against Desdemona, Othello becomes incoherent and unfocused, seemingly content to subscribe to the racial inferiority Iago has attributed to him, and referring to himself metaphorically as a 'turbanned Turk' (5.2.351) – in other words the very Ottomite he originally undertook to fight.

As these quotations indicate, the issue is not simply one of a binary opposition between Europeans and non-Europeans but of a whole range of subtle and fluid distinctions between racial, national and religious identities. Loomba argues that in most scholarship, 'religious prejudice was often distinguished much too drastically from racism, which meant that histories of Christian interactions with Jews and Muslims were neglected', and she pays attention to these interactions in her accounts of *Titus Andronicus* and *The Merchant of Venice*, two Shakespeare plays that feature prominent 'others'.[85] With reference to the former play, Loomba shows how the rise of the slave trade meant that the racial category of 'Moor' took on a new complexity. While medieval stereotypes of black villainy remained popular, in Shakespeare's era a distinction arose between North and Sub-Saharan Africans: 'North African or Arab Moors, being Muslim, are allowed a cultural lineage, religious traditions, and occasionally a lighter skin colour. Sub-Saharan Africans are increasingly associated with a lack of religion and culture, and painted as low-born'.[86] Thus the difference between the 'barbarous Moor' Aaron (2.2.78)[87] and Othello the 'noble Moor' (*Othello* 2.3.134) may not necessarily be attributable to developments in Shakespeare's sensibility or dramatic practice but rather to the availability of more complex discourses of race than had previously been assumed.[88] Equally the representation of Shylock in *The Merchant* is complicated by associations between Jews and Muslims, as well as 'heightened confusion about whether Jewishness was a nationality, a religion, or a race'.[89] While work in this area has proliferated at a huge rate in the last twenty years, Loomba's distinctive contribution to the debate is her concern with recovering early modern representations of race in texts and stage practices, with refusing to separate the analysis of racial, national and religious differences from the analysis of gender and sexuality, and in locating her analyses in her pedagogical practice and her identity as an Indian-born scholar. As she points out, 'teaching Shakespeare in a non-Western classroom is a daily reminder that it is impossible to divorce what cultural difference means "in" the plays from what it means in our lives'.[90]

Gender and sexuality

As Loomba argues, discourses of gender and sexuality cannot easily be separated from those of racial, religious and national identity, since 'patriarchal domination and gender inequality provided a model for establishing (and were themselves reinforced by) racial hierarchies and colonial domination'.[91] Each of the plays addressed in the previous section examines gender and sexuality alongside race, religion and nation: for example, one of the ways that Prospero justifies his treatment of Caliban is by referring to the latter's attempt to rape Miranda; Cleopatra's identity is sexualized from the first speech of the play; Othello's sexual relationship (or lack of it) with Desdemona is of course the material Iago uses to make him jealous; Aaron is having an affair with Tamora, queen of the Goths, who gives birth to his child; and *The Merchant of Venice* is shot through with fantasies about castration and miscegenation. Nevertheless, it is fair to say that cultural materialist work on Shakespeare has been particularly concerned with issues of gender and sexuality in their own right. I have touched upon questions of masculinity and homosexuality in previous chapters; however, a consideration of the role of feminism is long overdue. In fact, the issue of the space available for feminism within Shakespeare criticism, and cultural materialism in particular, has been the subject of very significant debate.

Sinfield points out that feminism and cultural materialism have a shared lineage; indeed 'cultural materialism is the outcome of a cross-fertilization with materialist feminism'.[92] Dollimore agrees, citing 'some of the major developments in feminism' as key influences on the approach.[93] There is not the room here to account for these developments and associations, nor to address the huge range of valuable work done on Shakespeare by feminist critics who do not subscribe to cultural materialism.[94] Nevertheless, I do want to pay attention to a revealing debate around feminism and cultural materialism that was prompted by Kathleen McLuskie's essay for *Political Shakespeare*. In a discussion of *Measure for Measure*, McLuskie argues that unless the play is subjected to a 'radical rewriting' there is no way in which a materialist feminist critic can gain purchase upon it:

> Feminist criticism of this play is restricted to exposing its own exclusion from the text. It has no point of entry into it, for the dilemmas of the narrative and the sexuality under discussion are constructed in completely male terms – gelding and splaying hold no terror for women – and the women's role as the objects of exchange within that system of sexuality is not at issue, however much a feminist might want to draw attention to it.[95]

Although the point about gelding and splaying, a threat made in *Measure for Measure*, ignores the fact that both words refer to the neutering of women as well as men, McLuskie's larger argument is convincing.[96] What pleasure can a feminist take, she asks, in a Shakespearean comedy that depends upon sexism and misogyny for its effects?[97] It might be a little difficult for us to think of *Measure for Measure* as a comedy, but the same point can be made about *The Taming of the Shrew* and *As You Like It*, both plays that, whatever else they might do to destabilize gender norms, also include moments of misogyny.[98] McLuskie detects the same problems in *King Lear*, particularly its representation of Goneril and Regan as ungrateful villains. However, here she offers a characteristically cultural materialist solution, arguing that feminism can be well served 'by making a text reveal the conditions in which a particular ideology of femininity functions'. The text then becomes not a statement of 'the world as it is', but a site in which ideas are shown to be under contestation, 'which would restore the element of dialectic, removing the privilege both from the character of Lear and from the ideological positions which he dramatizes, [which] is crucial to a feminist critique'.[99]

The American scholar Lynda E. Boose responded to McLuskie's account of the relationship between feminism and Shakespeare in an influential 1987 article. She sees McLuskie's essay as symptomatic of the approach of historicist-inflected political criticism of Shakespeare as a whole, which, she claims, always tends to contrive some way of silencing or limiting women.[100] While she calls McLuskie's argument 'tough, articulate, uncompromising, and identifiably British', Boose takes issue with her conclusion that feminism must either reject Shakespeare or reshape him. She comments, 'to be a feminist in McLuskie's terms is to renounce completely one's pleasure in Shakespeare and embrace instead the rigorous comforts of ideological correctness'.[101] What Boose sees as the implicit dichotomy between feminism and pleasure aligns the former with the sort of puritanical perspective that, in the early modern period, ultimately kept the theatres of the English Republic closed.[102] Dollimore takes up the argument in an essay that addresses a range of feminist criticisms of cultural materialism, and suggests that Boose's central opposition is false:

> what is at issue is not pleasure versus puritanism but different kinds of pleasure, different kinds of historical

inquiry, and different kinds of politics ... McLuskie is, in
the first instance, seeking to practice the responsibilities of
the historian as well as the commitment of the feminist, *and*
seeking to show that they are not incompatible.[103]

For Dollimore, a dissatisfaction with the representation of
women in Shakespeare does not cancel out the possibility of
enjoying the plays themselves. What has been neglected in this
argument, he notes, is 'the pleasure of subversion', a point that
leads him onto his playful version of *Antony and Cleopatra*
mentioned in the last chapter.[104] The aesthetic effect of
playfully subverting a pre-existing text is perhaps more easily
understood in terms of a twenty-first-century popular culture
that is saturated with the remix, the reboot and the adaptation.
While some critics bemoan the creative bankruptcy of such
practices, in fact the best appropriations take advantage of
the distance, ironic or not, between themselves and their
source texts in order to create pleasure for an audience that is
familiar with, but does not venerate, an original.[105]

In a sense this is a debate about Shakespeare and the politics
of authenticity. One way of being a feminist Shakespearean
is to, as Boose puts it, 'serve Shakespeare' by arguing that his
work transcends the stereotypes of his time and offers what
amounts to a proto-feminist presentation of women.[106] This
approach, which Sinfield refers to as 'collaboration', thus
preserves an 'authentic' Shakespeare, constructed as a mirror-
image of modern-day progressive politics, that can retain
his privileged place in culture as a source of wisdom and
authority.[107] This is of a piece with what Dollimore has called
'wishful theory', as discussed in Chapter 2.[108] McLuskie's alternative is to emphasize what might be called a personal sense
of political authenticity by remaining faithful to her feminist
principles and challenging those elements of Shakespeare that
uncritically recirculate misogynistic discourses. Clearly, each
of these positions can lead to 'the *affirmative habit* of literary
criticism', also discussed in Chapter 2, in which 'the critic
will indulge in whatever strenuous reading is necessary to

get the Shakespearean text onto his or her side'.[109] McLuskie is accused of this, I think unfairly, but the possibility exists in both camps. Even if that is avoided, if it is permissible for cultural materialists to read plays against the grain in order to draw out their political significance, the strategy is likewise open to those critics who are more optimistic about Shakespeare's position on gender politics. Such a reading only becomes problematic if it is not sufficiently historicized or if it locates the origin of progressive values in Shakespeare, the person, himself. McLuskie addresses the former problem when she argues, 'As a political movement, feminism is directed to social transformation ... That political aim cannot be served by asserting the timelessness of feminism, turning the struggles of early modern women into costume drama versions of our own.'[110] With regard to the latter issue, as I argued in Chapter 3, Shakespeare was an independent agent who grasped the significant dramatic potential of provocative ideas, but he was not a man out of time. For it is perfectly possible to detect the presence of proto-feminist ideas in Shakespeare's plays without falling back on 'the genius of Shakespeare'. In accordance with Williams's model of culture, competing ideas about women were circulating in the early modern period, and for every misogynistic text like Joseph Swetnam's *Araignment of Lewde, Froward and Inconstant Women* there was a rebuttal like Rachel Speght's *A Mouzell for Melastomus*.[111] McLuskie's argument is that a feminist analysis of Shakespeare should proceed from a materialist basis, and that it should guard against the temptation to explain away or, worse, to ignore those elements of his work that are misogynistic. As Dollimore puts it, instead the project 'follows the unstable constructions of, for example, gender and patriarchy back to the contradictions of their historical moment'.[112]

McLuskie's point about the feminist critic's exclusion from the Shakespearean text is picked up again by Sinfield in *Shakespeare, Authority, Sexuality*, where he uses it as a way of introducing his analysis of *The Merchant of Venice* that, as discussed in Chapter 3, proceeds from the question of whether Sinfield, as a gay man, is necessarily excluded from Shakespeare. There is much to commend what Sinfield calls his 'good gay reading' of *The Merchant*, in which he proposes, among other things, that in the life they live after the play has concluded, Portia and Antonio might share the affections of Bassanio.[113] For example, early modern households were large and conventionally included all sorts of hangers on; as Foucault argues, the concept of homosexuality did not yet exist in the way that it does for us, so binary views of sexuality were much less entrenched in Shakespeare's day; similarly the idea of companionate marriage was a new one, so to impose a modern-day version of married coupledom on to Bassanio and Portia would be to overlook the very real differences between our era and theirs.[114] By drawing out these historical differences, readings like Sinfield's remind us that Shakespeare's values were not necessarily ours, and in the process perform a two-fold service: the historical specificity of Shakespeare's work is revealed, and Shakespeare is interpreted anew for the contemporary era. Sinfield puts it like this:

It is not that Shakespeare was a sexual radical, therefore. Rather, the early-modern organization of sex and gender boundaries was different from ours, and the ordinary currency of that culture is replete with erotic interactions that strike strange chords today. Shakespeare may speak with distinct force to gay men and lesbians, simply because he didn't think he had to sort out sexuality in modern terms. For approximately the same reasons, these plays may stimulate radical ideas about race, nation, gender, and class.[115]

This approach also has the benefit of preserving the kind of progressive reading of Shakespeare that Boose is understandably reluctant to lose, while doing justice to the significance of early modern ideological formations.

If one of the tasks of cultural materialism is to pay attention to historical assumptions made about sexuality and gender, such attention can also bring the assumptions of our own era into sharper focus. In a notorious comment, Scott Wilson claims that with the advent of cultural materialism 'students are now being asked to read with their genitals'.[116] It is not entirely clear what Wilson means by this. He can't be referring to whether the student is gay, straight, bisexual or asexual (can he?), since the possession of genitals is no guide to that. Perhaps he means gender – but again that would be to ignore the well-known distinction between sex, which is a matter of biology, and gender, which is constructed ideologically. Surely he isn't talking about sexual excitement? (It's important to consider the pleasure of the text, but there are limits.) Wilson's confusion, or perhaps mine, demonstrates how clumsy our language of sexuality and gender can be. However, that language might become less clumsy, and therefore perhaps the experience of sexuality and gender themselves less fraught, when it is set alongside that of Shakespeare's era. In a discussion of Shakespeare's sonnets, Sinfield refers to four categories formulated by Esther Newton and Shirley Walton in the interests of 'women's sexual diversity and possibility':

> sexual preference (from which gender you usually select your partners);
> erotic identity (how you image yourself);
> erotic role (who you want to be in bed);
> and erotic acts (what you like to do in bed).[117]

Sinfield uses this scheme as part of his reading of the relationship between the poet and the young man in the sonnets, arguing that while the pair's desires align in the first two categories their preferences in the others make them a poor match. It is a long way from Wilson's blithe reference to 'genitals' to Newton and Walton's subtle erotics, and much further still to the world of desire that Shakespeare and his contemporaries lived in. Nevertheless, with scholarship, with imagination and with commitment, the past and the present are capable of reflecting some light on one another.

5

'The Nature of an Insurrection': Cultural Materialism and *Julius Caesar*

Shakesummer

It is the summer of 2016 and the temptation to retreat from the world into art is very strong. The news tells of terrible events on a seemingly daily basis: bloody and unrelenting conflict in Syria, the biggest refugee crisis since the Second World War, the deaths of hundreds in terrorist attacks, a rise in demagoguery and racially motivated violence, not to mention the unexpected deaths of gifted artists and entertainers. It is also the summer of Shakespeare. In the UK the 400th anniversary of his death is being marked by festivals, broadcasts and books. What better time to turn away from it all and embrace the bard? And yet, in the light of cultural materialism, such resignation could not be considered anything other than a failure. Once it is accepted that 'no cultural practice is ever without political significance', then the prospect of a retreat from the real world into the world of Shakespeare becomes impossible.[1] In difficult times it is certainly easier to understand the cry of the traditionalist who laments the supposed inability of the political critic to find Shakespeare 'spiritually restoring', but if all Shakespeare's works are good for is contemplation and consolation then we may as well canonize him and be done with it.[2] And as *Love's Labour's Lost* suggests, perhaps even that idea of academic retreat is a mirage, for no sooner do Ferdinand and his lords swear they will withdraw from the world than the world draws them back again. Whichever approach is taken, the coincidence of this *aestas horribilis* and Shakesummer has led to a remarkable cross-pollination: again and again, Shakespeare is being used by public figures, journalists and cultural commentators as a tool with which to read current events. As Terence Hawkes argues, that is always the case – '*we* mean *by* Shakespeare', as he says – yet the rate at which this is currently occurring is remarkable.[3] I will examine some of these instances in the third section of this chapter, in keeping with the cultural materialist interest in the ways that Shakespeare's work is made to speak in contexts far removed from its own historical moment. But beyond this, I will draw attention to a cultural materialist argument that has perhaps not received as much attention as it deserves. If literature does not just bear the marks of the culture that produced it but also makes an impact upon that culture itself, it is naive to think that such interventions will always be positive or even merely benign in nature. Despite his compulsory presence in every British classroom, his status as an icon of the UK's cultural 'soft power' and his location just this side of sainthood, Shakespeare is dangerous.

The classic expression of this idea is Walter Benjamin's: 'there is no document of civilization which is not at the same time a document of barbarism'.[4] Benjamin's point has perhaps been illustrated most clearly by critics who have paid attention to the way that Shakespeare represents and has been represented by colonial power. Yet Jonathan Dollimore offers another perspective on the relationship between literature and barbarity that further strikes at the notion that the works of Shakespeare necessarily have a beneficial influence upon their audience. Extending his critique of essentialist-universalist humanism, Dollimore argues that accounts of literature that stress its civilizing effect not only overlook all those who have historically been excluded from humanism based on their gender, race, sexuality, political views or other qualities, but also, and just as seriously, ignore aspects of the text that challenge humanist ideals in their own terms. As Dollimore puts it, 'many of the canonical works of literature claimed by and for the humanist vision so obviously threaten rather than confirm it ... the aesthetic vision has been most captivating precisely when it exceeds and maybe violates the humanitarian one'.[5] The point here is that a great deal of the literature that engages readers and audiences does so because it transgresses the limits of what is generally agreed to be humane behaviour, and does not necessarily condemn those transgressions. Dollimore stresses that this is a broad although not a universal claim:

> It is obviously more applicable to some genres, periods and movements where what is central is a dangerous knowledge of the dissident desires which threaten rather than what confirms psychic and social equilibrium, and prevailing notions of civilised life – e.g. Greek Tragedy, the drama of the English Renaissance (including Shakespeare's), the epics of that same period (especially those of Spenser and Milton), and countless nineteenth- and twentieth-century texts.[6]

Dollimore lists Milton's Satan, Shakespeare's Macbeth and a range of other protagonists as embodiments of threats to 'civilised life', and we might add to this list a great deal of the work that falls into today's horror, thriller and SF genres. While humanist criticism would typically argue that the disturbing actions of a Macbeth, an Iago or an Edmund are ultimately repudiated at the closure of the play in which they appear, cultural materialist readings have never given very much weight to endings. In other words, what matters is not the containment of disruptive forces at the conclusion of a Shakespeare play, but the release of those forces for some of its duration. So, for example, in *A Midsummer Night's Dream*, the control of adolescent sexuality represented by the marriages of Hermia to Lysander and Helena to Demetrius towards the end of the play cannot be seen to cancel out the challenges to conventional notions of sexual and gendered behaviour that the couples' earlier transgressive experiences in the forest represent. Dollimore's point is that the same principle when applied to the actions of a tragic protagonist leaves us with a reading of Shakespeare's plays which actively threatens values that humanists hold dear. Thus, in *King Lear*, Cordelia's restrained response to her father's request for an account of her love reveals 'how the laws of human kindness operate in the service of property, contractual, and power relations',[7] while in the temptation scene *Othello* becomes a 'sexual fantasy' that 'dramatizes a pornographic imagination ... central ... to a certain kind of ambivalent racism in which disgust and desire escalate dialectically'.[8] These are not the sorts of ideas around which commemorative festivals are usually organized.

It is important to register that Dollimore's attention to the danger of literature is not a turn to nihilism. His aim is not simply to lament the various depravities to which human beings can sink but, as Ewan Fernie puts it, to testify to the fact that 'literature speaks wild truth, which criticism will always evade'.[9] The political programme that arises from this 'wild truth' is thus the same one that has motivated cultural materialists from the very beginning, and which can be seen in Dollimore's rejection of 'wishful theory' and Alan Sinfield's dismissal of 'the affirmative habit': it lies in revealing the disconcerting and dialectical evidence that traditional essentialist–universalist humanism refuses to see. The result is a critical approach that reads Shakespeare unflinchingly, and as a way of revivifying the progressive political project. As Dollimore suggests, 'the ethical and the humane, in order not to atrophy, must be constantly exposed to their own vital exclusions – exposed, that is, to what allows them to be what they are'.[10] In what follows I will offer a cultural materialist reading of Shakespeare's *Julius Caesar* in order to consider the wild truth that it tells about the relationship between people and politics, to suggest how the play might have resonated in early modern England and to consider how it speaks, and has been made to speak, in the contemporary cultural climate.

But first I want to make a brief return to *King Lear* and to the summer of Shakespeare, dominated as it is by dire political events. The following quotation seems, in its own halting manner, to go some way towards identifying the danger that Dollimore sees in Shakespeare, before quickly retreating from the implications of that insight:

> Most of us have been exposed to the work of Shakespeare, and he spends a great deal of time dwelling on the characteristics of human nature. Some of the examples are extreme, but they aren't so far-fetched as to be unbelievable, or Shakespeare wouldn't still be performed today … One of his greatest achievements was *King Lear*, which is a good lesson in how good intentions don't always work out for the best, and it becomes a virtual wipeout while showing the complexities of human relations. That's a dark example, but it's better to be aware than to be unaware of what the world can be like.
>
> On the brighter side, I think most people want to be the best they can be. That's probably one reason you're reading this right now – you've chosen the high road, the path to more knowledge and experience.[11]

The passage above comes from a book called *Think Like a Champion: An Informal Education in Business and Life*, and its author is Donald J. Trump – or perhaps Meredith McIver, who is credited on the book's cover (in a much smaller font, naturally) as Trump's co-author. Either way, the reading of *King Lear* offered here is a revealing one. It begins in humanist platitudes, positing a Shakespeare who has especial access to a human nature that remains recognizable 400 years after his death, even if some of his representations test the boundaries of plausibility. Still, you can't argue with the box office, and if Shakespeare continues to sell tickets then he must have been on to something. We then enter the domain of Jan Kott who, as Sinfield points out, offers a nihilistic view of *King Lear* in which human nature is 'an unalterable given which political action cannot affect'.[12] Be careful who you deal with, Trump seems to say, because before you know it a perfectly reasonable three-way division of a business empire can result in a series of increasingly hostile takeover bids, temporary insanity and the deaths of several family members. Finally, there is a return to humanist optimism: people want to better themselves, and reading is a good way of doing that. Of course, in the context of Trump's book, being 'the best they can be' means 'being the richest they can be', a moment where humanism and consumerism are revealed as one and the same. These days, Trump's high road is the road to the White House, and I'll return to this later in the chapter. But what I'd most like to know about Trump's reading of *King Lear* is the point at which the play stopped being a warning about how badly human beings can treat each other – and thus an encouragement to think, however naively, about changing that – and became a template for a political campaign. Does the fact that Trump can see human relations as *either* 'a virtual wipeout' *or* a 'high road', but not both, tell us something about the democratic political process or Dollimore's concept of 'dangerous knowledge'? Is Trump speaking his own version of wild truth? With the aid of *Julius Caesar*, a play about factionalism, political legitimation and the cultivation of interpersonal relationships, I will offer some answers to these questions.

Past

Julius Caesar (1599) has always been troublesome. The conflicted motives of a series of complex characters – Brutus,

Cassius, Caesar, Antony – have generated centuries of disagreement. Moreover, the clash between an elitist republicanism and what amounts to a populist monarchism has led to the play being claimed for a range of political positions. Sinfield has suggested that 'the dominant attitude among modern humanities intellectuals' towards the play is one of balanced ambivalence: each character is both right and wrong, having compromised their private morality for what they see as a public good. Such a view, notes Sinfield, works to 'discourage political engagement'.[13] Such discouragement is ironic given the fact that *Julius Caesar* is a play that, if nothing else, dramatizes political engagement across the social spectrum. From the patrician elite to the common citizen, everyone in this play is interested in intervening in politics. And yet here more trouble lies, for most of those interventions construe political engagement as political violence. The play thus presents a puzzle to critics who would seek to salvage from it any model of positive human behaviour. No member of either the upper or lower classes of Rome seems to emerge with much dignity. Brutus may have been 'the noblest Roman of them all' (5.5.69), but his decision to allow Antony to speak in the aftermath of the assassination is just one of the reasons why he was also a catastrophically poor strategist.[14] Cassius is shown to have 'misconstrued everything' (5.3.84), while Caesar is either a tyrant-in-waiting or a narcissist whose claim to be 'constant as the northern star' (3.1.60) is laughable given his vacillation over whether to attend the senate on the morning of his assassination. Antony himself is a demagogue who does not shrink from condemning his brother-in-law to death if it will aid his own political ambition. As for the common people, they are a bloodthirsty 'rabblement' (1.2.243) happy to kill their compatriots almost indiscriminately. As Trump/McIver might say, it's a dark example.

Faced with this, it is no wonder that some critics despair of finding any positive political values in the play at all. According to Andrew Hadfield, 'Shakespeare represents Roman society as a toxic mixture of decayed republicanism and emergent tyranny', and the play is thus a bitter commentary on the lot of the disenfranchised Elizabethan citizen.[15] For the cultural materialists, Simon Barker is also pessimistic about the political process as it is represented in the play, but unlike Hadfield he suggests that that pessimism can at least be put to some contemporary use: 'we can *only* see *Julius Caesar* as inviting a severe critique of the power of rhetoric. It is an issue that concerns us daily in the modern world as much as it clearly concerned Shakespeare in his.'[16] John Drakakis, too, stresses the political usefulness of the play by reading it 'as an unmasking of the politics of representation per se' that we might recognize 'from our own media representations of a crisis',[17] while Graham Holderness and Marcus Nevitt use *Julius Caesar* 'to expose the manner in which right-wing government policy converts Shakespeare's play into an unambiguous text which advocates anti-populism and fetishises social hierarchy'.[18] For his part, Sinfield reads the play against the grain and offers two suggestions. First, that the tribunes Murellus and Flavius have the right idea when, acting like shop-stewards, they encourage the plebeians to 'assemble all the poor men of your sort' (1.1.58), an instruction that should be taken more seriously because 'lower-class and other dissident political groupings should be strengthened to resist the encroachments of the governing elite'.[19] Second, that the whole play can be imaginatively reconfigured as the dream of Cinna the poet, who in Sinfield's vision represents the modern intellectual who 'cannot jump out of ideology, but ... [has] a certain distinctive power – an ideological power – to write some of the scripts'.[20] In what follows, I will also seek to avoid counsels of despair by proposing ways in which *Julius Caesar* can be of some political use. My emphasis will be upon the sequence of historical differences that the play introduces between, first, its early modern production and its ancient setting and, second, that context of production and the current crisis of democracy that seems to be sweeping the US and the UK in the summer of 2016. In each case I will pay particular attention to representations of inter-class political affiliation as a way of locating, among the narcissism and demagoguery of the play, some progressive content. My aim in this first section is not to 'save' the play from the cynical political culture that it quite clearly espouses, but to reveal moments at which another resolution might have been possible. *Julius Caesar* is certainly a play in which, *pace* Dollimore, the ethical and the humane are constantly exposed to their own vital exclusions, but it is the former that I'd like, at least, to start with.

The first question that needs to be addressed about the status of *Julius Caesar* in its own time is how far early modern English culture was able to tolerate ideas of rebellion. As I've shown throughout this book, the cultural materialist position is that scope for such ideas was available but not easily found, and if it was found the difficulty of putting such ideas into practice was greater still. There is certainly plenty of evidence that the authorities were deeply concerned about the prospect of insurrection, and that they were determined to make use of the ideological apparatus of the state, namely the Church, in order to discourage it. One example of this is the 1570 'Homily against Disobedience and Wilful Rebellion', an authorized public sermon that churchmen were commanded to preach throughout the land. The information communicated in this sermon is clear and unambiguous:

> it is most evident that kinges, queenes, and other princes (for he speaketh of aucthoritie and power, be it in men or women) are ordayned of God, are to be obeyed and honoured of their subjectes; that such subjectes as are disobedient or rebellious against their princes disobey God and procure their owne damnation ... Is not rebellion the greatest of all mischeefes? And who are most redie to the greatest mischeefes, but the worst men?[21]

This kind of didactic address was grist to E. M. W. Tillyard's mill. But as Dollimore points out, 'didacticism was not the occasional surfacing, the occasional articulation, of the collective mind but a strategy of ideological struggle'.[22] And so it proves, since this particular homily was produced in the aftermath of a failed 1569 coup usually known as the Northern Rebellion, an attempt by Catholic earls from the north of England to replace Elizabeth I with Mary, Queen of Scots. Organized uprisings of national significance such as this were not an everyday occurrence, but neither were they particularly unusual in the period. As well as the 1601 Essex Revolt mentioned in the previous chapter, other significant insurrections in the period include the Pilgrimage of Grace (1536), the Prayer Book Rebellion (1549), Wyatt's Rebellion (1554), the abortive Oxfordshire Rising (1596), the Gunpowder Plot (1604) and of course the English Revolution (1642–9). In addition, small-scale rioting on a local level, often connected to agricultural issues such as crop failure or the forced enclosure of land, was so common as to be referred to by one historian as 'a national pastime'.[23]

There is some evidence that the authorities recognized the causes of such civil disobedience were not as straightforward as the 1570 homily might suggest, and that those that took part in rioting were not simply 'the worst men' disobeying the rule of God. In an account of the 1607 Midland Revolt against enclosure, Sir Roger Wilbraham notes how a group of more than 300 men from the counties of Warwickshire, Leicestershire and Northamptonshire spent twenty days 'throwing down the new enclosures' despite being offered clemency from the authorities if they desisted. Eventually, ten of the rioters were killed by mounted troops, and 'two or 3 were hanged as an example'. But in addition to these executions and the usual rhetoric about appealing against injustice through the proper channels, the Jacobean authorities recognized that the rioters might have had a genuine grievance. Wilbraham writes:

> the Judges of Assize, in order to satisfy the common people inveigh against Enclosers and Depopulators; and inquire concerning them and promise reformation at the hands of Justice. And this puts courage into the common people, so

that with mutterings they threaten to have a more violent revenge if they cannot be relieved. On this the Council appoints select Commissioners, learned in the law, in the six counties; to inquire concerning the acts of depopulation and conversion of arable into pasture land ... On this, directions were given to the learned counsel that the most notorious enclosers in each county should be summoned this Christmas for Hilary Term before the Star Chamber: and justice and mercy shown to them, so that they should not despair, nor should the common people insult them or be incited to make rebellion, whereof they are greatly suspected ... And it is hoped that this public example may stay the fury of the common people. These deliberations I reported to the King ... And he seems to approve of this course, for the manifestation of his justice and the speedy reformation of oppression.[24]

Such concessions were of course no use to the thirteen people who were killed when the uprising was put down, but, according to Wilbraham's account, while they condemn the rioting itself, authorities from the assize judges to the Privy Council and even the king himself agree that the rioter's cause was an important one. A revealing process of negotiation is at work here in the relationship between the commoners and the authorities. After the initial executions an inquiry is promised, which seems to embolden the people to threaten more violence. Next, Wilbraham says 'On this the Council appoints select Commissioners': the phrasing is ambiguous, but it is possible that such a threat encourages the authorities to take the investigation more seriously than had at first been envisioned. With the 'most notorious enclosers' called to the Star Chamber, justice is seen to be done, but the two-fold attitude of the authorities to the commoners is revealed: their obedience is both commanded ('Nor should the common people ...') and sought ('It is hoped ...'). This official reaction shows that it was possible, in some circumstances, for the early modern English state to conceive of a popular rebellion that was not purely sinful. Moreover, a form of negotiation takes place between the will of the people and the authority of the elite that is designed to result in an equitable solution to real injustice. While it is true that this relationship is backed on both sides by the threat of violence, the same can be said for virtually all other forms of negotiation between two or more powerful groups.

Contemporary works of political philosophy also offered support for the idea of a justified rebellion. Marian exiles such as John Knox, Christopher Goodman and John Ponet, together with later writers like Innocent Gentillet and George Buchanan, produced work diametrically opposed to the reactionary values espoused by the 'Homily against Disobedience'. This work, known collectively as resistance theory, argued that the citizen had every right to disobey the commandments of a corrupt governor or, in extreme cases, to overthrow and kill a tyrant. This passage by Ponet is indicative:

> This lawe testifieth to every mannes conscience, that it is naturall to cutte awaie an incurable membre which (being suffred) wolde destroie the hole body. Kinges, Princes, and other governours, albeit they are the headdes of a politike body, yet they are not the hole body. And though they be the chief membres, yet they are but membres: nother are the people ordained for them, but they are ordained for the people.[25]

Ideas like these were challenged and dismissed in their turn by more conservative thinkers; nevertheless, the question of insurrection was clearly a cultural faultline in Sinfield's terms: an issue on which the attitude of the ruling fraction 'fall[s] into contest and disarray'.[26] Famously, Shakespeare probes that faultline in *Coriolanus*, a play that unites Ponet's language of the body politic with the experience of food riots like the 1607 Midland Revolt. As Annabel Patterson has remarked, in *Coriolanus* 'the plebeians themselves (as distinct from their tribunes) are generously represented, and the popular voice, as

they themselves speak it, has genuine grievances to express'.[27]
Yet in *Julius Caesar*, that generosity seems to be lacking.

While there are significant moments of popular rebellion in *Henry VI, Part 2*, and Shakespeare seems to have written a scene in *Sir Thomas More* in which the eponymous character calms a potential riot, it is appropriate that two of the plays in which Shakespeare dramatizes civil unrest should be set in ancient Rome. As Coppélia Kahn points out, 'in relation to Renaissance England, Rome was as much a cultural parent as a cultural other', and this unique imaginative position meant that Rome could function as both exemplar and admonition.[28] Such ambivalence allowed a greater degree of scope for the exploration of troubling political ideas, and while Patterson offers a persuasive argument against reading the rebellious Jack Cade of *Henry VI, Part 2* as a simple tool of reactionary ideology, it is clear that she and other critics have found *Coriolanus* much easier to align with a sympathetic attitude towards lower class rebels.[29] In *Julius Caesar* that sympathy is hard to find, and the protective ambivalence of the Roman setting is primarily exploited as a means of investigating the ethics of not a popular revolt but an elite coup. The assassination of Julius Caesar functioned quite literally as a test case for resistance theory: the fame and complexity of the incident meant that it was used as a topic of debate in early modern English schools, as Freyja Cox Jensen attests: 'Caesar's death was itself the topic of schoolboy exercises: Melanchthon prescribed for discussion the question, "Was Brutus right or wrong in murdering Caesar?"'[30]

At stake here is what Robert Miola has called 'the tyrannicide debate'. With reference to ancient, medieval and early modern philosophy, Miola repeatedly demonstrates how Shakespeare's Caesar does and does not fit the mould of the confirmed tyrant, and how the conspirators do and do not fulfil the criteria of justified tyrannicides. Thus for Miola the play is, as Sinfield warns, a 'taut, balanced, and supremely ambivalent drama', no doubt the very reasons why the assassination made such a good classroom topic.[31] However, in a typical critical move, the complexity attributed to the motivations and behaviour of the elite characters is not granted to the lower classes, whose contradictions mark them out as merely 'fickle'. Miola emphasizes the need for tyrannicide to have the support of the people – the kind of democratic test that is much easier to dramatize in a Roman setting, where the voice of the people can plausibly be both celebrated and dismissed – but finds that they are not even capable of making a decision:

> Their vacillation in the Forum scene, wherein they change from doubt to admiration to anger, and their cruel fury toward Cinna the poet characterize them as dangerously unstable. These incidents render meaningless the question about whether the people consent (expressly or tacitly) to the assassination. Such consent could be only capricious whim.[32]

This is a demos that, even when it speaks, has no voice. Barbara Parker goes one step further than Miola in suggesting that the Roman people are not just dangerously capricious but actively tyrannical: 'Indeed, it may not be an overstatement to assert that the mob is the play's real protagonist, for they control not only Caesar and the other aristocratic characters but virtually the entire course of events.'[33]

Thus two discourses clash in *Julius Caesar*: the notion that tyrannicide might be justifiable in certain circumstances as long as it has popular consent, and the idea that the common people are not equipped to consent when those circumstances arise. Critics have suggested that the key difference between the plebeians and the elite can be understood in terms of their individuality. As Ian Munro points out, 'What separates the noble Romans from the many-headed monster is their lack of multiplicity: their small numbers and their individual names.'[34] Similarly, Jerald W. Spotswood argues,

> In denying commoners any level of status or any measure of individuality, which of course historically they did hold, Shakespeare rewrites individuality as a characteristic of the

elite and denigrates collective action by associating it with a rabble that by definition holds no interest in the social order.[35]

And yet, the first scene of the play does offer us a small group of commoners with a clear interest in the social order – albeit not the kind of interest that the members of the elite they encounter approve of – and one of whom, the Cobbler, is strongly individualized. The denomination 'Cobbler' is clearly an identification of the character's occupation, and thus offers some justification for the lack of lower class individuality critics have detected. However, it is worth noting that none of the characters that appear in this scene are referred to by name in the dialogue. Although the two tribunes of the people who also have speaking parts are named in the *dramatis personae*, in the stage directions at 1.1 ('*Enter* FLAVIUS, MURELLUS *and certain* Commoners *over the stage*', 0.1–0.2) and in the speech prefixes, their names are not spoken aloud until the following scene, when we learn that 'Murellus and Flavius, for pulling scarves off Caesar's images, are put to silence' (1.2.284–5). Thus unless an audience member had read the play in advance of seeing a performance, he or she would consider each speaker in this scene equally nameless. Moreover, most of the Cobbler's speeches are provocative quibbles upon his occupation, and thus could be read as assertions of individuality designed to mark him out as more than simply the work that he does:

MURELLUS	You, sir, what trade are you?
COBBLER	Truly, sir, in respect of a fine workman, I am but as you would say, a cobbler.
MURELLUS	But what trade are thou? Answer me directly.
COBBLER	A trade, sir, that I hope I may use with a safe conscience, which is indeed, sir, a mender of bad soles.
FLAVIUS	What trade, thou knave? Thou naughty knave, what trade?

> COBBLER   Nay I beseech you, sir, be not out with me: yet if you be out sir, I can mend you.
>
> MURELLUS   What mean'st thou by that? Mend me, thou saucy fellow?
>
> COBBLER   Why, sir, cobble you.
>
> FLAVIUS   Thou art a cobbler, art thou?
>
> COBBLER   Truly, sir, all that I live by, is with the awl: I meddle with no tradesman's matters, nor women's matters; but withal I am indeed, sir, a surgeon to old shoes; when they are in great danger, I recover them. As proper men as ever trod upon neat's leather have gone upon my handiwork.
>
>   (1.1.9–27)

The Cobbler's responses rely for their subversive humour on a series of puns, beginning with a self-deprecating quibble on 'cobbler'/'botcher' and continuing with the stock joke on the homophone 'soles'/'souls'.[36] As Tom Bishop notes, the Cobbler's verbal ingenuity shows up the tribunes' 'frustration at how signs and circumstances are slipping from their control', and their general hostility to the commoners reveals that although they have been elected to represent the interests of lower-class Romans, and were by law required to be of common birth themselves, Murellus and Flavius have long since turned their backs on their comrades.[37] However, the tribunes are also frustrated by the Cobbler's suggestion that he is able to 'mend their souls' or improve them spiritually. This is an impudent notion, but, as David Daniell suggests in his edition of the play, as well as its association with 'soles'/'souls', 'mend' may also imply a sexual offer, and indeed 'some of the heat in these exchanges is explained if *cobble* is also taken as "couple", a sense perhaps surviving in "cobble together"'.[38] In addition, it seems likely that 'awl'/'all' can be understood as 'penis' – as Jonathan Bate has convincingly argued in relation to this instance and Stephen Booth has suggested with reference to Shakespeare's sonnets – and 'meddle' and 'women's matters' also have sexual connotations.[39] Thus if, in his fifth speech, the Cobbler disclaims interest in 'women's matters' he may not be eschewing sexuality entirely, especially given the repetition of the 'awl' pun in 'withal' and the mention of 'proper men'. The latter phrase, in which 'proper' implies respectability as well as attractiveness, may again be a flirtatious reference to the tribunes. Whether the 'mending' that the Cobbler offers is spiritual, sexual or both, the character is clearly in command of the first half of the scene, and what he suggests is some sort of mutually beneficial relationship with the elite figures who encounter him. Murellus and Flavius, flustered, embarrassed and eventually incensed that the commoners are celebrating Caesar's triumph, reject this offer and revert to their positions of superiority, but two principles have nevertheless been established: that the lower-class characters can display individuality, and that the possibility of a positive relationship between the political classes and the commoners can exist if the commoners are allowed to express it. As the Cobbler illustrates, that individuality will not be deferent, but it might be all the more appealing for that. After all, we never hear Murellus's reply to the Cobbler's phrase 'Why, sir, cobble you'; instead, Flavius takes over the questioning in the next two exchanges. Is Murellus, silently, more interested in what might have been offered than he wishes to admit?[40]

An echo of this inclusive gesture can be found in the first scene of Act 2, where the conspirators formulate their plans for the assassination. In a soliloquy, Brutus offers a model of his thought process:

> Since Cassius first did whet me against Caesar
> I have not slept.
> Between the acting of a dreadful thing
> And the first motion, all the interim is
> Like a phantasma or a hideous dream:
> The genius and the mortal instruments
> Are then in council, and the state of man,

> Like to a little kingdom, suffers then
> The nature of an insurrection.
>
> (2.1.61–9)

Brutus clearly describes an unsettled state of mind here, and the speech has been read as a warning that civil war is the only possible result of the dangerous way that Brutus is thinking.[41] However, the insurrection with which the speech concludes is not necessarily something to be feared. Since the 'dreadful thing' Brutus refers to is the assassination he has by now decided it is right to undertake, it seems likely that 'dreadful' is being used to mean 'awe-inspiring' or 'formidable' rather than 'terrible'.[42] While 'hideous dream' develops the notion of sleeplessness by associating a sense of mental terror with the decision, the subsequent metaphor is more available for a positive reading. In Brutus's image of the human being as a microcosm of the nation, the animating metaphysical 'genius' is analogous to the ruling classes of Rome, while the material 'mortal instruments' of the body can be understood as the plebeians. Crucially, these two elements are not 'in conflict', a phrase Shakespeare could easily have used, but 'in council', hence reasoned and orderly debate is taking place. This then leads to the 'nature' of an insurrection, not the 'horror' of it or some other similar word; an unusual occurrence to be sure, but not one that is disastrous. Rather, there seems scope here to interpret the insurrection that Brutus imagines as an unprecedented but necessary and, in the metaphor at least, nonviolent realignment of ideas. Brutus achieves a revolutionary reformulation of his position – he has now decided to join with Cassius's conspiracy – and he understands that decision as analogous to the action of an insurrectionary force in which the elite join with the plebeians as equal partners. In accordance with Ponet's philosophy, the aim of that allied force is to benefit the social order as a whole through the justified removal of a tyrant. Such associations were not unheard of. Indeed, as Roger Manning points out, in contrast to most uprisings in Shakespeare's lifetime, the alliance of common people and gentry was a striking feature of some earlier insurrections:

During the late medieval popular revolts, by contrast, contact with the artisans of provincial towns and especially the inhabitants of London had produced a comparatively high degree of political awareness. In the rebellions of 1450 and 1536 the leadership provided by gentlemen also served to focus the attention of the protesters on larger issues, such as government policies initiated by unpopular royal ministers.[43]

Brutus's speech goes further in rejecting the vertical structure of the 1450 and 1536 revolts for a horizontal one where 'council' is the watchword, and confirms that such a thing is at least thinkable. Indeed, in Brutus's metaphor, such a thing is akin to the very process of thinking itself.

These two moments may have been produced by reading against the grain of the text, but as Wilbraham's account of the 1607 revolt shows, the idea of the elite and the commons forming a working relationship based on shared interests for progressive ends is not completely outlandish. In the case of *Julius Caesar*, we might see the conspirators as analogous to the assize judges and Privy Council members who were ultimately receptive to the will of the rioting commoners, while Caesar and his faction could stand in the place of the enclosers whose changes to the commonwealth were experienced as harmful. Of course, one of the characteristics of *Julius Caesar* is its facility for both anti- and pro-Caesarian readings, and in the Forum scenes of the play we see a crowd of common people taking against the conspirators, with dire consequences. It may be significant that while the Cobbler and his fellows in the first scene of the play are referred to in the stage directions as 'Commoners', those that appear in Act 3 Scene 2 are instead 'Plebeians', conceivably indicating that this latter episode is more securely located in ancient Rome than the former, which still kept one foot in early modern England. Perhaps it was easier – or less troubling – for Shakespeare to envisage a dangerously manipulable mob that was purely Roman in conception. Nevertheless, whereas the encounters I have been discussing proceed from a sense of mutual investment in, first, some form of beneficial interpersonal encounter, and, second, resistance theory, the plebeians who respond to Antony's oration in the Forum scene do so without making any meaningful contributions of their own. While at the beginning of the scene, as Holderness and Nevitt show, the plebeians demonstrate an interest in evaluating both the relative merits of Brutus and Cassius's speeches, and of Caesar and Brutus as heads of state, by the scene's end they have completely invested in the account of events that Antony has constructed for them.[44] For Naomi Conn Liebler, they are nothing more than a target market for Antony's sales patter; he, like 'a side-show mountebank, a hawker of fake cures ... literally commodifies Caesar's body as a collection of relics which he then peddles to the crowd'.[45] In a grotesque parody of the first scene of the play, the plebeians then encounter Cinna the poet who, like the Cobbler, finds himself on the streets in order to attend a ceremony connected with Caesar, in this case a funeral. Now it is the named patrician who must answer to the unnamed plebeians, and his very name is his downfall: the mob 'tear him to pieces' (3.3.28) even though they know he is not the Cinna they are looking for. This incident, one of the most disturbing moments in Shakespeare, fully justifies Dollimore's interest in the barbarous vision of literature, not least because the situation seems so familiar to us. In a perceptive analysis, Daniel Juan Gil reads this moment as the revenge of the nameless on the named, and suggests that 'this mob wants to reduce names to bodies'. He then goes on to offer a chilling reading of the scene's end that develops Liebler's emphasis upon the commodification of the body:

It is unclear whether Cinna survives this assault ... But if he survives and walks (or is even dragged) off stage, it could look, from the vantage point of the theatre audience, as though Cinna has been absorbed into the mob. It is of course only as theater – the theater Antony loves – that violence can stand for a mode of sociability that operates at the level of bodies.[46]

Despite Gil's caveat, it strikes me that this image of violence as social unity is not limited to the theatrical plane. Terribly, in the words of Antony, 'Mischief, thou art afoot: / Take thou what course thou wilt' (3.2.251–2). Welcome to 2016.

Present

In the television series *The Walking Dead* (2010–present), a programme that attracts a global following and up to 17 million American viewers, zombies are everywhere. Brainless, relentless and utterly devoid of empathy, they roam the countryside in search of human flesh, much of which they tear from the limbs of their unfortunate victims. As scholars have argued, zombies are the mob, the rabblement, the headless multitude who seek only to satiate their hunger for death.[47] They are, in other words, clear descendants of the plebeians who demand to 'be satisfied' (3.2.1) and thus eviscerate Cinna or, in Gil's reading, consume or assimilate him. For the two-fold threat of the zombie is to become their food, or to die and become them – and to become them means becoming part of the crowd. George A. Romero's film *Dawn of the Dead* has probably done the most to assure the status of the zombie as a satirical tool in popular culture. In a key sequence, the reanimated dead lumber aimlessly around an abandoned shopping centre while a human onlooker suggests that the zombies visit the mall out of 'some kind of instinct, memory. What they used to do. This was an important place in their lives.'[48] For Romero, the crowd was made up of zombified shoppers seeking the goods that mass-market advertising told them to desire; for Shakespeare, the plebeians who appear in Act 3 of *Julius Caesar* seek death and destruction because they have been sold Antony's account of a Caesar who loved the people but was cut down by envious conspirators. Both crowds are constituted as crowds by their shared sole aim for violent consumption. For the zombie, *pace* Gil, violence is a mode of sociability that operates at a bodily level, indeed the zombie crowd is purely corporal, utterly self-less. While a bite from a vampire might lead to a life of vicious bloodsucking, the victim will at least preserve their individuality; for the zombie, all such sense of self evaporates.

And yet in recent years a strain of revisionist zombie literature has conceived of zombies that can, to a certain extent, think, feel and love. In Isaac Marion's 2010 novel *Warm Bodies* (later a 2015 film), a teenage male zombie called 'R' retains enough of his selfhood to fall in love with a young human woman called Julie, much to the disgust of her father – a clear homage to *Romeo and Juliet*.[49] While Marion's book concludes with a tentatively happy ending for the star-crossed lovers, Laurie Rozakis's zombie *Romeo and Juliet* offers a resolution more in keeping with the original play's genre. In her faux study-guide *Zombie Notes*, Rozakis offers a Juliet who is passionately in favour of zombie rights, 'believing that zombies had an alternative – but entirely valid – worldview'.[50] Although she finds love with an undead but not quite zombified Romeo, tragically Juliet is forced to kill him when he becomes a fully fledged zombie. Her parting words are:

> O churl! I used to support zombie rights, but this is too gross.
> My honor'd parents were right about the undead;
> They are not fit to sleep with, much less wed.[51]

The imaginative leap that *Warm Bodies* takes is prefigured by Romero's emphasis on the status of the zombie as both the other and the same, but in moving from zombie as monster to zombie as lover Marion exercises the kind of extension of empathy that has been at the core of claims for the universalism of Shakespeare. *Warm Bodies* is thus in some ways a zombie extrapolation of Shylock's 'If you prick us, do we not bleed?' speech. But just as scholars of *The Merchant of Venice* have shown that the play does not live up to the egalitarian ideals espoused in that speech, so cultural materialists have argued that under close scrutiny all claims to the universalism of the bard begin to look like nothing other than pure assimilation.[52] For Rozakis's Juliet, the 'wishful theory' of the zombie rights movement falters when she comes face to face with a real zombie, and the only insight offered by this version of the play is that parents know best. Here we can see two ways in which rewritings of Shakespeare entwine with cultural myths of the other: in Marion's, a being that is first seen as nothing other than a (decaying) body can ultimately be loved at the expense of one's closest kin; in Rozakis's, the other will always remain the other, and righteousness is invested in the same. I would suggest that both of these disturbing approaches to otherness constitute Dollimore's category of 'dangerous knowledge'. In one formulation of this idea, Dollimore has remarked, 'If we want young people to read Shakespeare, let's attach to him a warning to the effect that he can damage psychic and moral health.'[53] In other words, let's treat Shakespeare in the same way that *Dawn of the Dead* was treated on its original release, for, as Roger Ebert notes in his review of the film, 'Nobody ever said art had to be in good taste.'[54] Whatever they might say about taste, the trouble with these versions of *Romeo and Juliet* is that their dangerous constructions of the relationship between the other and the same are not contained in an aesthetic world separate from the one in which we live. Instead, they bespeak and take part in their own culture, a culture in which questions of otherness and sameness are currently being asked with increasing desperation.

Zombies do not shuffle along twenty-first-century streets, but the polarization of political discourse that seems to be a pronounced characteristic of twenty-first-century life sometimes makes it feel as though they do. In public debate it appears more and more difficult for political opponents to concede that those with different views might actually be human, let alone have a point. If the claims of both sides in the Brexit debate were taken at face value, the choice of the United Kingdom to remain in or leave the European Union would lead either to the destruction or the salvation of Britain. Those who declared they would vote to leave were called racists while 'remainers' were accused of treachery. After the vote the two main British political parties were thrown into turmoil, and while the Conservatives emerged united from a brief leadership contest full of political duplicity and dramatic reversals, the Labour party embarked on a long process of in-fighting in which one side was characterized as 'Blairite scum' and the other 'Trotskyite entrists'. But this was not – and never is – just rhetoric: these were 'struggle[s] in and for representation' that had bloody ends.[55] On the same day that a poster featuring a photograph of a line of hundreds of refugees and the slogan 'Breaking Point' was unveiled by Nigel Farage, the leader of the UK Independence Party, the pro-Remain MP Jo Cox was assassinated by a gunman shouting 'Britain First', who later gave his name in court as 'death to traitors, freedom for Britain'. In the five days following the Brexit vote, reports of racially motivated attacks in the UK rose by 57 per cent according to the National Police Chiefs' Council.[56] Concurrently, in America, depending on who was to be believed, the next president would either be a murderous criminal or a fascist. The Republican candidate Donald Trump was promising, if elected, to build a wall on the Mexican border in order to prevent illegal immigration, and to ban all foreign-born Muslims from entering the country at all. White US police officers seemed to be shooting black men for no other reason than that they were black men. At the same time, across the world, terrorists claiming affiliation to ISIS, to far-right groups, or to their own private causes were indiscriminately killing innocent people in the name of, as Cassius has it, 'freedom, liberty and enfranchisement' (3.1.81). The bloody bodily sociability metaphorized by the Roman plebeians and the modern zombie is present in many of these acts, where violent rhetoric and actual violence are used to unite one group of people against another in a gesture of seemingly unbridgeable division.

Julius Caesar has been a popular lens through which some of these contemporary political events have been structured and interpreted. When Boris Johnson, *de facto* leader of the Leave campaign in the EU referendum and potential Prime Ministerial candidate, did not receive the support of his ally Michael Gove – who then stood for the job of PM himself – references to the play were not difficult to find. At the beginning of a speech that concluded with the announcement that he was not, after all, going to run for the position, Johnson paraphrased Brutus's well-known lines to Cassius about seizing opportunities when they arise: 'There is a tide in the affairs of men / Which, taken at the flood, leads on to fortune' (4.3.216–17). In Johnson's hands this became a validation of the Brexit decision as 'a time not to fight against the tide of history, but to take that tide at the flood and sail on to fortune', thus placing Johnson in the role of the post-assassination Brutus determined to capitalize upon the political climate that he has brought about.[57] By the time the speech had ended, it was Gove, not Johnson, who was the Brutus-figure. When asked for a comment about Gove's decision, Johnson's father replied '*Et tu, Brute?* is my comment on that. I don't think he's called Brutus but you never know.'[58] As Althusser warned, in lines that are just as appropriate to Brutus's attempt to manipulate anti-authoritarian public opinion as they are to Johnson's,

> the men who would use an ideology purely as a means of action, as a tool, find that they have been caught by it, implicated by it, just when they are using it and believe themselves to be absolute masters of it.[59]

Three weeks later at the Republican National Convention, Donald Trump accepted the party's presidential nomination in an address beginning 'Friends, delegates, and fellow Americans', an obvious echo of the opening words of Antony's oration over Caesar's corpse. Trump also mimicked Antony's speech by making great use of pathos. Compare Antony:

> then burst his mighty heart;
> And in his mantle muffling up his face,
> Even at the base of Pompey's statue,

Which all the while ran blood, great Caesar fell.
O what a fall was there, my countrymen!
Then I, and you, and all of us fell down,
Whilst bloody treason flourished over us.
O, now you weep, and I perceive you feel
The dint of pity.

(3.2.184–92)

And Trump:

nothing has affected me more deeply than the time I have
spent with the mothers and fathers who have lost their
children to violence spilling across our border ... My
opponent will never meet with them, or share in their pain
... These wounded families have been alone. But they are
alone no longer. Tonight, this candidate and this whole
nation stand in their corner to support them.[60]

While Antony focuses on the body of Caesar to bring the
already sympathetic plebeians to fever pitch, Trump uses the
grief of parents whose children were killed by undocumented
immigrants in road accidents and a mistaken-identity shooting
to represent himself as the defender of the innocent and
paint his opponent Hillary Clinton as a heartless traitor. In
both extracts, an appeal to national unity takes place over
literal or metaphorical bodies, a tactic calculated to bring
about a visceral sense of sociability especially among those
who hear the speech in person. However, Trump's canniest
rhetorical strategy is not borrowed from Antony, but, perhaps
surprisingly, from Murellus and Flavius – or at least from the
positions they held in the Roman polity. When Trump says 'I
am your voice', a claim he makes in the middle of the speech
and repeats again at its conclusion, he is taking on the role of
tribune of the people. Thus, like Johnson, Trump fulfils a dual
position in the imagined afterlife of *Julius Caesar*: he styles
himself as both Antony the proto-dictator and Murellus the
supposed representative of the people.

The two-fold positions that Johnson and Trump adopt reveal the reason for their rise and the danger that they embody. Posing as Brutus and Caesar, Johnson was able to represent himself as both rebel and authoritarian, as someone who while willing to ride the flood tide of anti-EU sentiment in order that the British people might 'take back control', as the Leave slogan proclaimed, was at the same time content to exploit for personal advantage the connections he made through attendance at Eton and Oxford as well as, notoriously, membership of the elite Bullingdon Club. Despite being born into wealth and privilege, Trump styles himself as a self-made Murellus who rails against the system and says the unsayable, whether or not it has any basis in truth. And as Antony he can claim insider knowledge of the political process due to decades of bankrolling, and hobnobbing with, representatives and senators. By disguising their 'insideness' as 'outsideness', Johnson and Trump are able to appeal across the lines that ordinarily divide those uninterested in politics from the political process itself and to use the demagoguery of Shakespeare's Caesar and Antony, coupled with the revolutionary fervour of Brutus and Murellus, to help them do it. Both figures like to represent themselves as speaking 'wild truth' – of saying what others are too afraid to say because of so-called 'political correctness'. But to dignify the rhetoric that emanates from these camps with the name of truth would be grotesque, and to position oneself against political correctness is to believe that there is a mode of life that can be lived outside of politics, that the personal is not political. The falsehoods upon which both the Leave campaign and the Trump presidential candidacy have been run thus remind us of something that *Julius Caesar* warns against: democracy is by its very nature open to exploitation, and a tyrant who is able to persuade a crowd of people, perhaps even the majority of an electorate, to agree with them is no less a tyrant if their platform is based on lies and the demonization of the other. This is the wild truth that the play tells, the dangerous knowledge that must be disinterred from it in every new performance and re-reading. Trump's candidacy in particular offers clear sight of the ethical and humane because those are the very qualities missing from his speeches and interviews, thus giving support to Dollimore's contention that such exclusions, however repellent, can be valuable.[61] Since *Julius Caesar* was produced under a political system that understood democracy as a hazard to be guarded against at all costs, it is able to reveal the pitfalls of that system to us with no embarrassment. Indeed, Shakespeare's representation of Murellus and Flavius accomplishes something like that by itself. Here are two 'men of the people', elected by the people to serve them, who reject their responsibilities in favour of elite political factionalism. Far from the shop-stewards envisaged by Sinfield, they are none other than Johnson and Trump: supposed representatives of the people who have no allegiance to anything other than their own ambition.

Future

The solution that *Julius Caesar* offers to the problem of demagoguery is tentative and fragile. As I have suggested, it depends upon reading the Cobbler in 1.1 and Brutus' speech at 2.1.61–9 as indicative of a progressive alliance between those with power and those without. This was a difficult, though not unprecedented idea in early modern England, and the play's representation of Roman tribunes of the people demonstrates a scepticism that it can be put into practice even when formalized by a constitution. Yet over the last few years there have been reasons for hopefulness. Movements like Occupy Wall Street, Black Lives Matter, 38 Degrees and Momentum have sought to advocate progressive political positions of social justice with some success, and many setbacks. As *Julius Caesar* suggests, they will only succeed if the barrier between the people and those with power to effect change can be meaningfully and ethically broken.

Sinfield warns against reading *Julius Caesar* as a way of interpreting contemporary party politics because that approach 'maintains the media fiction that Washington infighting is the necessary and adequate site of political activity'.[62] He may well be right, and to that end I have sought to emphasize the crucial possibility of political action that the play opens up for the plebeians, although of course it also has a less optimistic story to tell about their role in politics. Nevertheless, in his 'dream of Cinna the poet', Sinfield posits that 'the dream and nightmare of modern intellectuals [is] that they are invited to feast with Caesar, to become significant in government'.[63] An alternative version of this dream is staged in the 2016 Coen Brothers film *Hail, Caesar!* Set in 1930s Hollywood, the film shows how a famous actor played by George Clooney is kidnapped by a group of communists calling themselves 'the future' and persuaded, with very little effort on the part of the communists, to use his star power to help the radical cause. This latter dream seems to me the more accurate one: the contemporary academic both dreads and longs to be called to serve the political cause of the anti-establishment. But both versions of this fantasy fall foul of the egotism that brings down Caesar, Brutus, Cassius and, in the end, Antony. Perhaps a better dream is the one represented by the Globe Theatre's 2016 Word by Word project. In this venture, a typewriter connected to Twitter automatically types out Shakespeare's complete works by sourcing each word from tweets published online in real time. As the press release has it:

> Since not all of Shakespeare's language will be found in real time Tweets, the typewriter will stop when it cannot find the next word – at which point, the public will be asked to help out by tweeting it themselves, using the hashtag #TheCompleteTweets.[64]

This is one way of democratizing Shakespeare, and a metaphor for political participation on a horizontal axis that precludes a descent into anarchy due to its collectively identified goal. It is a form of crowdsourcing perhaps even Cinna could get behind.

APPENDIX

Podcasts interviews with the authors of most of the titles in the *Arden Shakespeare and Theory* series are available. Details are listed below.

Available titles

Shakespeare and Cultural Materialist Theory, Christopher Marlow
http://blogs.surrey.ac.uk/shakespeare/2016/11/04/shakespeare-and-contemporary-theory-31-shakespeare-and-cultural-materialist-theory-with-christopher-marlow/

Shakespeare and Ecocritical Theory, Gabriel Egan
http://blogs.surrey.ac.uk/shakespeare/2016/05/20/shakespeare-and-contemporary-theory-24-shakespeare-and-ecocritical-theory-with-gabriel-egan/

Shakespeare and Ecofeminist Theory, Rebecca Laroche and Jennifer Munroe
http://blogs.surrey.ac.uk/shakespeare/2016/06/07/shakespeare-and-contemporary-theory-25-shakespeare-and-ecofeminist-theory-with-rebecca-laroche-and-jennifer-munroe/

Shakespeare and Economic Theory, David Hawkes
http://blogs.surrey.ac.uk/shakespeare/2016/05/05/shakespeare-and-contemporary-theory-22-shakespeare-and-economic-theory-with-david-hawkes/

Shakespeare and New Historicist Theory, Neema Parvini
http://blogs.surrey.ac.uk/shakespeare/2016/08/29/shakespeare-and-contemporary-theory-27-shakespeare-and-new-historicist-theory-with-evelyn-gajowski-and-neema-parvini/

Forthcoming titles

Shakespeare and Feminist Theory, Marianne Novy
http://blogs.surrey.ac.uk/shakespeare/2016/05/13/shakespeare-and-contemporary-theory-23-shakespeare-and-feminist-theory-with-marianne-novy/

Shakespeare and Film Theory, Scott Hollifield
http://blogs.surrey.ac.uk/shakespeare/2016/10/28/shakespeare-and-contemporary-theory-30-shakespeare-and-film-theory-with-scott-hollifield/

Shakespeare and Postcolonial Theory, Jyotsna Singh
http://blogs.surrey.ac.uk/shakespeare/2016/07/19/shakespeare-and-contemporary-theory-26-shakespeare-and-postcolonial-theory-with-jyotsna-singh/

Shakespeare and Posthumanist Theory, Karen Raber
http://blogs.surrey.ac.uk/shakespeare/2016/09/30/shakespeare-and-contemporary-theory-28-shakespeare-and-posthumanist-theory-with-karen-raber/

Shakespeare and Presentist Theory, Evelyn Gajowski
http://blogs.surrey.ac.uk/shakespeare/2016/04/29/shakespeare-and-contemporary-theory-21-the-arden-shakespeare-and-theory-series-with-evelyn-gajowski/

Shakespeare and Queer Theory, Melissa E. Sanchez
http://blogs.surrey.ac.uk/shakespeare/2016/10/18/shakespeare-and-contemporary-theory-29-shakespeare-and-queer-theory-with-melissa-e-sanchez/

NOTES

Introduction

1 Jonathan Dollimore, 'Introduction: Shakespeare, Cultural Materialism and the New Historicism'. In *Political Shakespeare: Essays in Cultural Materialism*, eds Jonathan Dollimore and Alan Sinfield, 2nd edn (Manchester, 1994), 2–17 (10).

2 Jonathan Dollimore and David Jonathan Y. Bayot, *Jonathan Dollimore in Conversation* (Manila, 2013), 20.

3 Jonathan Dollimore and Alan Sinfield, 'Foreword to the First Edition: Cultural Materialism'. In Dollimore and Sinfield, eds, *Political Shakespeare*, vii–viii (vii).

4 Alan Sinfield, *Cultural Politics – Queer Reading*, 2nd edn (London, 2005), viii.

5 Alan Sinfield, *Shakespeare, Authority, Sexuality: Unfinished Business in Cultural Materialism* (Oxford, 2006), 2.

6 Hugh Grady, 'Shakespeare Studies, 2005: A Situated Overview', *Shakespeare* 1 (2005): 102–20 (110–12). This trend has also been remarked upon by Jonathan Gil Harris, 'The New New Historicism's *Wunderkammer* of Objects'. *European Journal of English Studies* 4 (2000): 111–23; Douglas Bruster, *Shakespeare and the Question of Culture: Early Modern Literature and the Cultural Turn* (Basingstoke, 2003), 191–206; Evelyn Gajowski, 'The Presence of the Past'. In *Presentism, Gender and Sexuality in Shakespeare*, ed. Evelyn Gajowski (Basingstoke, 2009), 1–22 (7); and Cary DiPietro and Hugh Grady, 'Introduction'. In *Shakespeare and the Urgency of Now: Criticism and Theory in the 21st Century*, eds Cary DiPietro and Hugh Grady (Basingstoke, 2013), 1–8 (4).

7 Jonathan Gil Harris, *Untimely Matter in the Time of Shakespeare* (Pennsylvania, 2009), 5.

8 Graham Holderness, *Cultural Shakespeare: Essays in the Shakespeare Myth* (Hatfield, 2001), 28.

Chapter 1

1 Goodreads claims to have more than 50 million members. http://www.goodreads.com/about/us (accessed 27 April 2016).

2 https://www.goodreads.com/author/quotes/947.William_Shakespeare (accessed 27 April 2016).

3 William Shakespeare, *As You Like It*, ed. Juliet Dusinberre (London, 2006).

4 John Webster, *The Duchess of Malfi*, ed. Leah S. Marcus (London, 2009).

5 William Shakespeare, *Julius Caesar*, ed. David Daniell (London, 1998).

6 The popularity of this accurate version of the quotation may be explained by its partial use as the title of John Green's bestselling young adult book, later a successful film, *The Fault in Our Stars*. In this version, the phrase is used as a synonym for 'star-crossed', and the novel depicts two *Romeo and Juliet*-style doomed lovers whose relationship is ended not by family conflict but by terminal illness.

7 This slogan is itself a popular misquotation of the last three sentences of the English translation of Karl Marx and Friedrich Engels, *The Communist Manifesto*, trans. Samuel Moore (London, 1967), 120–1. The lines read: 'The proletarians have nothing to lose but their chains. They have a world to win. WORKING MEN OF ALL COUNTRIES, UNITE!'

8 See William Shakespeare, *Pericles*, ed. Suzanne Gossett (London, 2004).

9 G. C. Macaulay, ed., *The Complete Works of John Gower*, 4 vols (Oxford, 1901), vol. 3, 268, ll. 1292–4.

10 Jonathan Dollimore, 'Introduction: Shakespeare, Cultural
Materialism and the New Historicism'. In *Political
Shakespeare: Essays in Cultural Materialism*, eds Jonathan
Dollimore and Alan Sinfield, 2nd edn (Manchester, 1994), 3.
The phrase appears throughout the work of Dollimore and
Sinfield including, in slightly different versions, Sinfield,
*Shakespeare, Authority, Sexuality: Unfinished Business
in Cultural Materialism* (Oxford, 2006), 3; Dollimore,
*Radical Tragedy: Religion, Ideology and Power in the
Drama of Shakespeare and his Contemporaries*, rev. 3rd edn
(Basingstoke, 2010), 288; Dollimore, *Sex, Literature and
Censorship* (Cambridge, 2001), 37; and Dollimore and David
Jonathan Y. Bayot, *Jonathan Dollimore in Conversation*
(Manila, 2013), 45. Marx's original version is usually
translated as 'Men make their own history, but they do
not make it just as they please; they do not make it under
circumstances chosen by themselves, but under circumstances
directly encountered, given and transmitted from the
past.' Marx, *The Eighteenth Brumaire of Louis Bonaparte*
(Moscow, 1934), 10.

11 William Shakespeare, *King Henry IV Part 1*, ed. David Scott
Kastan (London, 2002).

12 G. L. Kittredge, ed., *The Complete Works of Shakespeare*
(Boston, 1936), quoted in Daniell, ed., *Julius Caesar*, 172.

13 See 2.1.53–4.

14 I address this debate at length in Chapter 3.

15 Alan Sinfield, 'Introduction: Reproductions, Interventions'. In
Dollimore and Sinfield, eds, *Political Shakespeare*, 157. The
'e' missing from the end of the word 'note' seems to have been
transposed so that it appears eight lines earlier, to create the
phrase 'conservative drage [*sic*]'.

16 Dollimore, *Radical Tragedy*, 271.

17 William Shakespeare, *The Taming of the Shrew*, ed. Barbara
Hodgdon (London, 2010).

18 Ann Thompson notes a similar encounter in which 'one
female student who had studied *The Taming of the Shrew*
for Advanced Level told me that she had specifically been
taught how irrelevant modern feminism was to any reading

of the play'. See '*King Lear* and the Politics of Teaching Shakespeare', *Shakespeare Quarterly* 41 (1990): 139–46 (143).

19 The classic works on this issue are Joan Kelly, *Women, History and Theory* (Chicago, 1986) and *Rewriting the Renaissance: The Discourses of Sexual Difference in Early Modern England*, eds Margaret W. Ferguson, Maureen Quilligan and Nancy Vickers (Chicago, 1986). See also *A Feminist Companion to Shakespeare*, ed. Dympna Callaghan, 2nd edn (Oxford, 2016).

20 Dollimore, *Sex, Literature and Censorship*, 108.

21 Jonathan Dollimore and Alan Sinfield, 'History and Ideology: The Instance of *Henry V*'. In *Alternative Shakespeares*, ed. John Drakakis (London, 1985), 206–27 (206).

22 E. M. W. Tillyard, *The Elizabethan World Picture* (Harmondsworth, 1943), repr. 1968, back cover.

23 Ernest Mandel, 'Introduction'. In Karl Marx, *Capital: A Critique of Political Economy*, vol. 1, trans. Ben Fowkes (London, 1976), 11–84 (54). Italics in original.

24 Ibid., 1024.

25 Dollimore, 'Introduction'. Dollimore and Sinfield, eds, *Political Shakespeare*, 5.

26 William Shakespeare, *Troilus and Cressida*, ed. David Bevington (London, 1998).

27 Tillyard, *The Elizabethan World Picture*, 19.

28 Ibid., 38.

29 Ibid., 37.

30 Ibid., 103.

31 Ibid., 121–2.

32 Ibid., 124.

33 E. M. W. Tillyard, *Shakespeare's History Plays* (Harmondsworth, 1944), 18.

34 This distinction is pointed out in, ironically, James Joyce's *Ulysses*, when Stephen Daedalus notes that the speaker of the phrase 'put money in thy purse' is Iago, not Shakespeare. See James Joyce, *Ulysses* (London, 1992), 37.

35 From an interview with Terry Coleman, *Guardian*, 5 September 1983, quoted in Margot Heinemann, 'How Brecht Read Shakespeare'. In Dollimore and Sinfield, eds, *Political Shakespeare*, 226–54 (227).

36 Heinemann, 'How Brecht Read Shakespeare', 227.

37 Ibid.

38 Catherine Belsey, *A Future for Criticism* (Oxford, 2011), 102.

39 John Drakakis, 'Afterword: The Next Generation'. In *Alternative Shakespeares*, vol. 2, ed. Terence Hawkes (London, 1996), 238–44 (244).

40 Tillyard, *The Elizabethan World Picture*, 70.

41 Ibid.

42 Gabriel Egan, *Shakespeare and Marx* (Oxford, 2004), 65.

43 Tillyard, *The Elizabethan World Picture*, 74.

44 William Shakespeare, *King Lear*, ed. R. A. Foakes (London, 1997).

45 Tillyard, *The Elizabethan World Picture*, 77.

46 Ibid.

47 I discuss postcolonial readings of *The Tempest* in Chapter 4.

48 Tillyard, *Shakespeare's History Plays*, 311.

49 Ibid., 318.

50 Ibid., 313.

51 Ibid.

52 Dollimore and Sinfield, 'History and Ideology', 216.

53 Ibid., 216–17.

54 Ibid., 226–7.

55 William Shakespeare, *King Henry V*, ed. T. W. Craik (London, 1995).

56 John Drakakis, '"Fashion It Thus": *Julius Caesar* and the Politics of Theatrical Representation'. In *Materialist Shakespeare: A History*, ed. Ivo Kamps (London, 1995), 280–91 (283).

57 Dollimore and Sinfield, 'History and Ideology', 217.

58 Ibid., 225.

59 Ibid.

60 Raymond Williams, *Keywords: A Vocabulary of Culture and Society*, 2nd edn (London, 1983), 138–9. In *Marxism and Literature* (Oxford, 1977) and *Culture* (Glasgow, 1981), Williams went on to develop a much more nuanced understanding of form that took account of its implication in social processes. However, his work in this area has not made much of an impression on the mainstream of cultural materialism.

61 Drakakis, 'Introduction'. In Hawkes, ed., *Alternative Shakespeares*, 12.

62 Terry Eagleton, *The Function of Criticism: From 'The Spectator' to Post-Structuralism* (London, 1984), 9.

63 Ibid., 80.

64 Eagleton's solution to the problem is to call for a criticism that sounds very much like cultural materialism itself: 'the contemporary socialist or feminist critics must be defined by an engagement in the cultural politics of late capitalism'. Ibid., 123.

65 Cleanth Brooks, 'The Formalist Critics'. *Kenyon Review* 13 (1951): 72–81 (72).

66 Alan Sinfield, *Faultlines: Cultural Materialism and the Politics of Dissident Reading* (Oxford, 1992), 74.

67 Jonathan Dollimore and Alan Sinfield, 'Culture and Textuality: Debating Cultural Materialism'. *Textual Practice* 4 (1990): 91–100 (97).

68 Terry Eagleton, *Literary Theory: An Introduction*, 2nd edn (Oxford, 1996), 43.

69 Pierre Macherey, *A Theory of Literary Production*, trans. Geoffrey Wall (London, 2006), 88. Italics in original.

70 G. Wilson Knight, *The Wheel of Fire: Interpretations of Shakespearian Tragedy*, 4th edn (London and New York, 2001), xi.

71 Ibid., 136.

72 Ibid., 146

73 Ibid.

74 Michel Foucault, *Power/Knowledge: Selected Interviews and Other Writings 1972–1977*, ed. Colin Gordon, trans. Colin Gordon et al. (Hemel Hempstead, 1980), 117.

75 Wilson Knight, *The Wheel of Fire*, 147–8.

76 Sinfield, *Faultlines*, 8.

77 Graham Holderness and Marcus Nevitt, 'Major Among the Minors: A Cultural Materialist Reading of *Julius Caesar*'. In '*Julius Caesar': New Critical Essays*, ed. Horst Zander (New York and London, 2005), 257–69 (258).

78 Ibid.

79 Ibid., 258–9.

Chapter 2

1 Keith Johnson, *Shakespeare's English: A Practical Linguistic Guide* (London, 2013), 41.

2 Carol Thomas Neely, 'Constructing the Subject: Feminist Practice and the New Renaissance Discourses'. *English Literary Renaissance* 18 (1988): 5–18 (6). In a footnote, Neely confesses the term 'somewhat inaccurately elides the two discourses' but notes 'for my purposes, the similarities are more important than the differences'.

3 Neema Parvini, *Shakespeare and Cognition: Thinking Fast and Slow through Character* (Basingstoke, 2015), 3.

4 Edward Pechter, *What Was Shakespeare? Renaissance Plays and Changing Critical Practice* (Ithaca, 1995), 69.

5 Jeremy Hawthorn, *Cunning Passages: New Historicism, Cultural Materialism and Marxism in the Contemporary Debate* (London, 1996), 4.

6 John Drakakis, 'Cultural Materialism'. In *The Cambridge History of Literary Criticism, vol. IX: Twentieth-Century Historical, Philosophical and Psychological Perspectives*, eds Christa Knellwolf and Christopher Norris (Cambridge, 2001), 43–58 (47).

7 Jonathan Dollimore and Alan Sinfield, 'Foreword to the First

Edition: Cultural Materialism'. In *Political Shakespeare: Essays in Cultural Materialism*, eds Jonathan Dollimore and Alan Sinfield, 2nd edn (Manchester, 1994), vii–viii (vii).

8 Stephen Greenblatt, *Learning to Curse: Essays in Early Modern Culture* (New York and London, 1990), 146.

9 Stephen Greenblatt, *Renaissance Self-Fashioning: From More to Shakespeare* (Chicago, 1980), 4–5. Italics in original.

10 Dollimore and Sinfield, 'Foreword', viii.

11 See Louis Adrian Montrose, '"Shaping Fantasies": Figurations of Gender and Power in Elizabethan Culture'. *Representations* 2 (1983): 61–94.

12 Catherine Gallagher and Stephen Greenblatt, *Practicing New Historicism* (Chicago, 2000), 48.

13 Montrose observes that the phrase cultural poetics 'more accurately represents the critical project commonly known as new historicism': 'Professing the Renaissance: The Poetics and Politics of Culture'. In *The New Historicism*, ed. H. Aram Veeser (New York and London, 1989), 15–36 (17).

14 Kiernan Ryan, *New Historicism and Cultural Materialism: A Reader* (London, 1996), xv.

15 Gallagher and Greenblatt, *Practicing New Historicism*, 9.

16 Ibid., 8.

17 Ibid.

18 Pierre Macherey, *A Theory of Literary Production*, trans. Geoffrey Wall (London, 1978), 103.

19 Ibid., 106.

20 Ibid., 69.

21 Alan Sinfield, *Faultlines: Cultural Materialism and the Politics of Dissident Reading* (Oxford, 1992), 45.

22 Ibid., 49.

23 Alan Sinfield, *Cultural Politics – Queer Reading*, 2nd edn (London, 2005), 28.

24 John Drakakis, 'Terminator 2½: Or Messing with Canons'. *Textual Practice* 7 (1993): 60–84 (72). Italics in original.

25 Dollimore and Sinfield, 'Foreword', viii.

26 See Catherine Belsey, 'Towards Cultural History – in Theory and in Practice'. *Textual Practice* 3 (1989): 159–72 (172 n.16).

27 Dollimore, 'Introduction: Shakespeare, Cultural Materialism and the New Historicism'. In Dollimore and Sinfield, eds, *Political Shakespeare*, 2–17 (13).

28 Belsey, 'Towards Cultural History', 165. Italics in original.

29 See especially Jacques Derrida, *Positions*, trans. Alan Bass (Chicago, 1971) and *Margins of Philosophy*, trans. Alan Bass (Chicago and London, 1982).

30 Belsey, 'Towards Cultural History', 166.

31 Ibid., 165.

32 Jonathan Dollimore and Alan Sinfield, 'Culture and Textuality: Debating Cultural Materialism', *Textual Practice* 4 (1990): 91–100 (91).

33 Ibid., 92.

34 Ibid., 93.

35 Jonathan Dollimore, *Sex, Literature and Censorship* (Cambridge, 2001), 38.

36 Catherine Belsey, *A Future for Criticism* (Oxford, 2011), 18–19.

37 Sinfield, *Faultlines*, 8.

38 Dollimore and Sinfield, 'Culture and Textuality', 98.

39 Ibid., 99.

40 Variations of this kind of approach can be seen in the work of critics such as Simon Barker, Michael D. Bristol, John Drakakis, Evelyn Gajowski, Hugh Grady, Terence Hawkes, Graham Holderness, Ania Loomba and many others.

41 Alan Sinfield, 'Give an Account of Shakespeare and Education, Showing Why You Think They Are Effective and What You Have Appreciated About Them. Support Your Comments with Precise References'. In Dollimore and Sinfield, eds, *Political Shakespeare*, 158–81 (178).

42 Alan Sinfield, *Shakespeare, Authority, Sexuality: Unfinished Business in Cultural Materialism* (Oxford, 2006), 25.

43 The quotation used in the sub-heading is from Dollimore and Sinfield, 'Culture and Textuality', 98.

44 Dollimore, 'Introduction'. In Dollimore and Sinfield, eds, *Political Shakespeare*, 2.

45 Greenblatt, *Learning to Curse*, 2.

46 John Higgins, *Raymond Williams: Literature, Marxism and Cultural Materialism* (Oxford, 1999), 6.

47 Raymond Williams, *Marxism and Literature* (Oxford, 1977), 2.

48 Ibid., 83.

49 Raymond Williams, *Culture and Society 1780–1950* (London, 1990), 281.

50 Williams, *Marxism and Literature*, 80.

51 Ibid., 171–2.

52 Raymond Williams, 'Notes on Marxism in Britain Since 1945'. In *Culture and Materialism: Selected Essays* (London, 1980), 233–51 (243).

53 Ibid. In the introduction to *Marxism and Literature*, Williams defines cultural materialism as 'a theory of the specificities of material cultural and literary production within historical materialism', and notes that it differs from what is usually understood as Marxist theory (5).

54 Higgins, *Raymond Williams*, 135.

55 Dollimore and Sinfield, 'Foreword'. In Dollimore and Sinfield, eds, *Political Shakespeare*, vii.

56 Gallagher and Greenblatt, *Practicing New Historicism*, 62.

57 Williams, *Marxism and Literature*, 122.

58 Ibid., 123.

59 Ibid.

60 Ibid., 122.

61 Sinfield, *Shakespeare, Authority, Sexuality*, 7.

62 William Shakespeare, *King Henry V*, ed. T. W. Craik (London, 1995).

63 See Thomas Elyot, *The Book Named the Governor*, ed. S. E. Lehmberg (London, 1962), 133–48; Thomas Peacham,

The Compleat Gentleman (Oxford, 1906), 39–40. I discuss the impact of these ideas on early modern academic culture in *Performing Masculinity in English University Drama, 1598–1636* (Farnham, 2013), esp. chs 1 and 4.

64 See Alan Bray, 'Homosexuality and the Signs of Male Friendship in Elizabethan England'. In *Queering the Renaissance*, ed. Jonathan Goldberg (Durham, NC, 1994), 40–61.

65 For an accessible history of the friendship tradition, see A. C. Grayling, *Friendship* (New Haven and London, 2013).

66 See Alan Bray, *The Friend* (Chicago, 2003), esp. chs 1 to 4.

67 Bruce R. Smith, *Homosexual Desire in Shakespeare's England: A Cultural Poetics* (Chicago, 1991), 265.

68 Francis Bacon, *The Major Works*, ed. Brian Vickers (Oxford, 2002), 391.

69 Sinfield, *Faultlines*, 134, 136; also published in John Drakakis, ed., *Alternative Shakespeares* (London, 1985), 206–27.

70 Ibid., 142.

71 Ibid., 138–9.

72 Sinfield, *Shakespeare, Authority, Sexuality*, 91–2. My italics.

73 Ibid., 91–2.

74 Ibid., 198. Italics in original.

75 Don E. Wayne, 'Power, Politics and the Shakespearean Text: Recent Criticism in England and the United States'. In *Shakespeare Reproduced: The Text in History and Ideology*, eds Jean E. Howard and Marion F. O'Connor (London, 1987), 47–57 (52).

76 Catherine Belsey, 'Historicizing New Historicism'. In *Presentist Shakespeares*, eds Hugh Grady and Terence Hawkes (London, 2007), 27–45 (43).

77 Jonathan Dollimore and Alan Sinfield, 'History and Ideology: The Instance of *Henry V*'. In *Alternative Shakespeares*, ed. John Drakakis (London, 1985), 206–27 (216–17).

78 It appeared in *Glyph* 8 (1981), 40–61; *Political Shakespeare*, 18–47; *Shakespeare's 'Rough Magic': Renaissance Essays in Honor of C. L. Barber*, eds Peter Ericsson and Coppélia Kahn (Newark, NJ, 1985), 276–302; and Stephen Greenblatt,

Shakespearean Negotiations (Berkeley, 1988), 21–65. I refer to the version in Dollimore and Sinfield, eds, *Political Shakespeare*.

79 Stephen Greenblatt, 'Invisible Bullets: Renaissance Authority and its Subversion, *Henry IV* and *Henry V*'. In Dollimore and Sinfield, eds, *Political Shakespeare*, 18–47 (23–4).

80 Ibid., 30.

81 Ibid., 33.

82 Ibid., 45.

83 Carolyn Porter, 'Are We Being Historical Yet?' *South Atlantic Quarterly* 87 (1988): 743–86 (764–5). Italics in original.

84 Steven Mullaney, *The Place of the Stage: License, Play and Power in Renaissance England* (Chicago and London, 1988), 9; 31. Italics in original.

85 Porter, 'Are We Being Historical Yet?', 781.

86 Jonathan Dollimore, *Sexual Dissidence: Augustine to Wilde, Freud to Foucault* (Oxford, 1991), 85.

87 Greenblatt, 'Invisible Bullets', 45.

88 Dollimore, *Sex, Literature and Censorship*, 45.

89 Sinfield, *Faultlines*, 29.

90 Greenblatt, *Learning to Curse*, 165.

91 Montrose, 'Professing the Renaissance', 22.

92 Jonathan Dollimore and David Jonathan Y. Bayot, *Jonathan Dollimore in Conversation* (Manila, 2013), 15.

Chapter 3

1 Terence Hawkes, *Meaning by Shakespeare* (London and New York, 1992), 4.

2 Jonathan Bate, *The Genius of Shakespeare* (London, 1997), 257.

3 William Shakespeare, *Hamlet*, eds Ann Thompson and Neil Taylor (London, 2006).

4 For a detailed discussion of these issues, see the Arden 2
Hamlet, ed. Harold Jenkins (London, 1982), 484–90.

5 See Eric P. Levy, *Hamlet and the Rethinking of Man* (Madison,
2008), 108–20, and Brian P. Copenhaver and Charles B.
Schmitt, *Renaissance Philosophy* (Oxford, 1992), 260–71.

6 Jonathan Dollimore, 'The Legacy of Cultural Materialism'.
Textual Practice 27 (2013): 715–24 (723).

7 Neema Parvini, 'Reply to Jonathan Dollimore'. *Textual
Practice* 27 (2013): 724–33 (725).

8 Neema Parvini, *Shakespeare and Contemporary Theory: New
Historicism and Cultural Materialism* (London, 2012), 132.
Italics in original.

9 Dollimore, 'The Legacy of Cultural Materialism', 716. His
preferred replacements, idealism and materialism, are used
extensively by cultural materialists and throughout this study.

10 Jonathan Dollimore, *Radical Tragedy: Religion, Ideology and
Power in the Drama of Shakespeare and his Contemporaries*,
reissued 3rd edn (Basingstoke, 2010), 258.

11 Jonathan Dollimore, *Sexual Dissidence: Augustine to Wilde,
Freud to Foucault* (Oxford, 1991), 26.

12 See Gayatri Chakravorty Spivak, *In Other Worlds: Essays in
Cultural Politics* (London and New York, 1987), 270–304.

13 Alan Sinfield, *Shakespeare, Authority, Sexuality: Unfinished
Business in Cultural Materialism* (Oxford, 2006), 198.

14 Jean-Paul Sartre, *Existentialism and Humanism*, trans. Philip
Mairet (London, 2007), 54. Italics in original.

15 Karl Marx, *Selected Writings in Sociology and Social
Philosophy*, eds T. B. Bottomore and Maximilien Rubel
(Harmondsworth, 1963), 67.

16 Kate Soper, *Humanism and Anti-Humanism* (London, 1986),
18.

17 Alan Sinfield, *Faultlines: Cultural Materialism and the Politics
of Dissident Reading* (Oxford, 1992), 291.

18 Paul Kurtz, ed., *The Humanist Alternative* (London, 1973),
65; quoted in Soper, *Humanism and Anti-Humanism*, 11.

19 Soper, *Humanism and Anti-Humanism*, 11. Dollimore

identifies a similar misunderstanding when he notes that some critics 'failed completely to distinguish the British Marxist tradition from the French Althusserian one'. See Dollimore and David Jonathan Y. Bayot, *Jonathan Dollimore in Conversation* (Manila, 2013), 20.

20 Marx, *Selected Writings*, 83. Italics in original.

21 Jonathan Dollimore, 'Introduction: Shakespeare, Cultural Materialism and the New Historicism'. In *Political Shakespeare: Essays in Cultural Materialism*, eds Jonathan Dollimore and Alan Sinfield, 2nd edn (Manchester, 1994), 3.

22 Neema Parvini, *Shakespeare's History Plays: Rethinking Historicism* (Edinburgh, 2012), 113.

23 Jonathan Dollimore, 'A Response to Neema Parvini'. *Textual Practice* 27 (2013): 733–5 (733). Italics in original.

24 Jan Kott is chiefly remembered by scholars for his book *Shakespeare Our Contemporary*, which appeared in English translation in 1967. The book reads Shakespeare in the light of Kott's experiences in Stalinist Poland, emphasizing the irresistible power of history and the futility of human existence. Wilbur Sanders's *The Dramatist and the Received Idea* (1968) shares Kott's view of history but suggests that meaning can be found in the individual's attempt to preserve their personal integrity.

25 Sinfield, *Faultlines*, 112. This chapter of Sinfield's book is co-authored by Dollimore.

26 Ibid., 113.

27 Ibid., 114.

28 Ibid., 125.

29 Ibid., 320, n.11.

30 Parvini, *Shakespeare's History Plays*, 113; quoted in Parvini, 'Reply', 724.

31 John Donne, *The Major Works*, ed. John Carey (Oxford, 1990), 344.

32 Alan Sinfield, 'Heritage and the Market, Regulation and Desublimation'. In Dollimore and Sinfield, eds, *Political Shakespeare*, 255–79 (259). Italics in original.

33 See, for example, the 1598 'Proclamation against Vagabonds

and Unlawful Assemblies', the 1601 'Proclamation Licensing Casper van Senden to Deport Negroes' and Joseph Swetnam, *An Arraignment of Lewd, Idle, Froward and Unconstant Women* (London, 1615).

34 Andrew Milner, *Re-Imagining Cultural Studies: The Promise of Cultural Materialism* (London, 2002), 84. Italics in original.

35 Louis Althusser, 'Ideology and Ideological State Apparatuses'. In *Lenin and Philosophy and Other Essays*, trans. Ben Brewster (London, 1971), 145. Italics in original.

36 Althusser, 'Ideology', 165–7.

37 Ibid., 159. Italics in original.

38 Ibid., 161.

39 Ibid., 162.

40 Catherine Belsey notes the 'uneasy distinction' between these two versions of ideology in 'Towards Cultural History – in Theory and in Practice'. *Textual Practice* 3 (1989): 159–72 (165).

41 Althusser, 'Ideology', 171. Italics in original.

42 Raymond Williams, 'Notes on Marxism in Britain Since 1945'. In *Culture and Materialism: Selected Essays* (London, 2005), 233–51 (245).

43 Louis Althusser, *For Marx*, trans. Ben Brewster (London, 2005), 233.

44 Althusser, 'Ideology', 174.

45 Dollimore, 'Introduction'. In Dollimore and Sinfield, eds, *Political Shakespeare*, 2–17 (2).

46 Michel Foucault, *The Order of Things: An Archaeology of the Human Sciences* (London, 1970), 387.

47 Michel Foucault, *The History of Sexuality Volume I: An Introduction*, trans. Robert Hurley (London, 1981), 101.

48 Michel Foucault, *Power/Knowledge: Selected Interviews and Other Writings, 1972–1977*, ed. Colin Gordon (Hemel Hempstead, 1980), 98.

49 Althusser, 'Ideology', 181.

50 Ibid., 157.

51 Catherine Belsey, 'Historicizing New Historicism'. In *Presentist Shakespeares*, eds Hugh Grady and Terence Hawkes (London, 2007), 27–45 (38).

52 Parvini suggests that Althusser 'would account for ideologies that do not work for the current state as being those of bygone epochs (or old states), as being ultimately outmoded ideologies. This is an argument Althusser never makes but it is implicit in his system' (*Shakespeare and Contemporary Theory*, 70), which sounds very much like Williams's notion of residual cultural forms.

53 Soper, *Humanism and Anti-Humanism*, 110.

54 Foucault, *History of Sexuality*, 95–6. Italics in original.

55 Brent L. Pickett, 'Foucault and the Politics of Resistance'. *Polity* 28 (1996): 445–66 (464–5).

56 Althusser, 'Ideology', 128.

57 Dollimore, *Sexual Dissidence*, 282.

58 William Shakespeare, *Troilus and Cressida*, ed. David Bevington (London, 1998).

59 Althusser, *For Marx*, 234. Italics in original.

60 Dollimore, *Sexual Dissidence*, 89.

61 Hubert L. Dreyfus and Paul Rabinow, *Michel Foucault: Beyond Structuralism and Hermeneutics* (Brighton, 1982), 187–8. The authors cite a personal communication from Foucault. Quoted in Soper, *Humanism and Anti-Humanism*, 140.

62 William Shakespeare, *Julius Caesar*, ed. David Daniell (London, 1998).

63 William Shakespeare, *Macbeth*, eds Sandra Clark and Pamela Mason (London, 2015).

64 Dollimore, *Sexual Dissidence*, 88.

65 Raymond Williams, *Politics and Letters: Interviews with New Left Review* (London, 1979), 252.

66 Sinfield, *Faultlines*, 42. My italics.

67 Dollimore, *Sexual Dissidence*, 81. My italics.

68 Alan Sinfield, 'How to Read *The Merchant of Venice* Without Being Heterosexist'. In *Alternative Shakespeares*, vol. 2, ed.

Terence Hawkes (London, 1996), 122–39 (123). Reprinted in Sinfield, *Shakespeare, Authority, Sexuality*, 53–67.

69 Terence Hawkes, *That Shakespeherian Rag* (London and New York, 1986), 1.

70 Jonathan Dollimore, 'Shakespeare, Cultural Materialism, Feminism and Marxist Humanism'. *New Literary History* 21 (1990): 471–93 (489–90). A version of this essay, with the names of the academics removed, appears as Chapter 7 of the second edition of *Political Shakespeare*.

71 Dollimore, 'The Legacy of Cultural Materialism', 721.

72 Sinfield, *Shakespeare, Authority, Sexuality*, 15. I return to this example in Chapter 4.

73 Parvini, *History Plays*, 46.

74 Sinfield, *Shakespeare, Authority, Sexuality*, 198.

75 Alan Sinfield, *Cultural Politics – Queer Reading*, 2nd edn (London, 2005), viii.

76 Sinfield, *Shakespeare, Authority, Sexuality*, 20.

77 The game's homepage is http://gamebookadventures.com/gamebooks/to-be-or-not-to-be/ (accessed 6 July 2016).

78 If the option is chosen nevertheless, the player is told 'Listen, I'm going to cut our losses here. You're not allowed to be Ophelia for a while.'

79 Sinfield, *Faultlines*, 37.

Chapter 4

1 William Shakespeare, *King Henry V*, ed. T. W. Craik (London, 1995).

2 William Shakespeare, *King Richard III*, ed. James R. Siemon (London, 2009).

3 Ben Jonson, 'To the Memory of My Beloved, The Author, Master William Shakespeare, and What He Hath Left Us'. In William Shakespeare, *The Complete Works*, eds John Jowett et al., 2nd edn (Oxford, 2005), lxxi–lxxii, ll. 43, 77.

4 'I.M.S.', 'On Worthy Master Shakespeare and his Poems'. In ibid., lxxiii, ll. 1–4.

5 Jonathan Dollimore, 'Introduction: Shakespeare, Cultural Materialism and the New Historicism'. In *Political Shakespeare: Essays in Cultural Materialism*, eds Jonathan Dollimore and Alan Sinfield, 2nd edn (Manchester, 1994), 2–17 (10).

6 Catherine Belsey, *The Subject of Tragedy* (London, 1985), 5.

7 For the connection between Essex and Shakespeare, see *King Richard II*, ed. Charles R. Forker (London, 2002), 9–16.

8 Dermot Cavanagh neatly summarizes the ways in which Essex's motivations have been read: on the one hand, 'it may be misguided to impute ... any subtlety of interest, beyond that of an apparently successful deposition, in the spectacle of Shakespeare's play'; on the other, 'the play's dialectical openness ... may have been the source of a more complex interest from the Essex circle'. See Cavanagh, 'The Language of Treason in *Richard II*'. *Shakespeare Studies* 27 (1999): 134–60 (156).

9 E. K. Chambers, *William Shakespeare: A Study of Facts and Problems*, 2 vols (Oxford, 1930), vol. 2, 326.

10 Antony Sher and Gregory Doran, *Woza Shakespeare! Titus Andronicus in South Africa* (London, 1996), 212–13. I owe this reference to Siân Adiseshiah.

11 Esther Cloudman Dunn, *Shakespeare in America* (New York, 1939), 247–8.

12 Terence Hawkes, *Meaning by Shakespeare* (London, 1992), 3. Italics in original.

13 Ibid. Italics in original.

14 Michael Bristol, *Big-Time Shakespeare* (London and New York, 1996), 27.

15 Jonathan Dollimore and Alan Sinfield, 'Foreword to the First Edition: Cultural Materialism'. In Dollimore and Sinfield, eds, *Political Shakespeare*, vii–viii (vii).

16 See, for example, James Shapiro, *Shakespeare and the Jews*, 20th anniversary edn (New York and Chichester, 2016),

and William Shakespeare, *The Merchant of Venice*, ed. John
Drakakis (London, 2011).

17 Alan Sinfield, *Shakespeare, Authority, Sexuality: Unfinished
Business in Cultural Materialism* (London and New York,
2006), 22.

18 Jonathan Dollimore, *Sex, Literature and Censorship*
(Cambridge, 2001), 170.

19 Louis Althusser, 'Ideology and Ideological State Apparatuses'.
In *Lenin and Philosophy and Other Essays* (London, 1971),
162.

20 David Scott Kastan, *Shakespeare After Theory* (New York and
London, 1999), 16–17.

21 Hugh Grady and Terence Hawkes, 'Presenting Presentism'. In
Presentist Shakespeares, eds Hugh Grady and Terence Hawkes
(London and New York, 2007), 1–5 (2).

22 Ibid., 4.

23 Nevertheless, the so-called 'presentist' work of a great many
critics continues to pay attention to such sources.

24 Evelyn Gajowski, 'The Presence of the Past'. In *Presentism,
Gender and Sexuality in Shakespeare*, ed. Evelyn Gajowski
(Basingstoke, 2009), 1–22 (8).

25 Lucy Munro, 'Shakespeare and the Uses of the Past: Critical
Approaches and Current Debates'. *Shakespeare* 7 (2011):
102–25 (116).

26 Sinfield, *Shakespeare, Authority, Sexuality*, 22. In 'Shakespeare
Studies, 2005: A Situated Overview'. *Shakespeare* 1 (2005):
102–20, Grady acknowledges that cultural materialism, along
with new historicism and several other critical methodologies,
is an 'instance of presentist practice' (114). Grady's account
of presentism in this essay owes a great deal to cultural
materialism; indeed, if Dollimore's description of cultural
materialism as 'an evolving project' is accepted, Grady's
presentism *is* cultural materialism. See Jonathan Dollimore and
David Jonathan Y. Bayot, *Jonathan Dollimore in Conversation*
(Manila, 2013), 20.

27 John Drakakis, 'Cultural Materialism'. In *The Cambridge
History of Literary Criticism, vol. IX: Twentieth-Century*

Historical, Philosophical and Psychological Perspectives, eds Christa Knellwolf and Christopher Norris (Cambridge, 2001), 43–58 (46).

28 Helen Taylor, 'Leaving Parties and Legacies: Reflections across the Binary Divide on a Decade of Englishes'. In *The State of Theory*, ed. Richard Bradford (London, 1993), 42–56 (48).

29 Martin Blocksidge, 'Shakespeare: Iconic or Relevant?' In *Shakespeare in Education*, ed. Martin Blocksidge (London, 2003), 1–19 (11).

30 For a brief account of these changes see Stefan Collini, *What are Universities For?* (London, 2012), 20–38; for their current implications, see Andrew McGettigan, *The Great University Gamble: Money, Markets and the Future of Higher Education* (London, 2013).

31 Helen Taylor, '"Are We Talking About Literature?" A History of LTP'. *LTP: Journal of Literature Teaching Politics* 6 (1987): 7–12 (12), quoted in Taylor, 'Leaving Parties and Legacies', 49.

32 We should not, however, get too complacent. Reading articles from *LTP* today, it is striking both how much and how little things have changed. Cultural materialism is now a more or less accepted critical methodology, but it is often presented to students on survey modules as one approach among many; they are invited to 'test drive' it for a week or two before it can be put safely away again. Having said that, as a straight white man, albeit from a working-class background, it is undoubtedly much easier for me to introduce politics into my teaching than it is for many of my colleagues. And as powerful as they were in 1982, the voices pronouncing the irrelevance of English in 2016 are even louder and this time, at least in the UK, they have a funding system biased against the humanities to assist them.

33 Isobel Armstrong, 'Thatcher's Shakespeare?' *Textual Practice* 3 (1989): 1–13 (1).

34 Simon Barker and others, 'Editorial'. *LTP: Journal of Literature Teaching Politics* 1 (1982): 1–3 (1).

35 Jonathan Dollimore, 'Then and Now'. *Critical Survey* 26 (2014): 61–82 (66).

36 See Holly Goulden and John Hartley, 'Nor Should Such Topics as Homosexuality, Masturbation, Frigidity, Premature Ejaculation or the Menopause be Regarded as Unmentionable'. *LTP: Journal of Literature Teaching Politics* 1 (1982): 4–20.

37 Alan Sinfield, 'Four Ways with a Reactionary Text'. *LTP: Journal of Literature Teaching Politics* 2 (1983): 81–95 (82).

38 Ibid., 91.

39 Charles H. Frey, *Experiencing Shakespeare: Essays on Text, Classroom, and Performance* (Columbia, MO, 1988), 141.

40 Alan Sinfield, 'Give an Account of Shakespeare and Education, Showing Why You Think They are Effective and What You Have Appreciated About Them. Support Your Comments with Precise References'. In Dollimore and Sinfield, eds, *Political Shakespeare*, 158–81 (159).

41 Ibid., 162, 164.

42 Ibid., 174.

43 Alan Sinfield, 'Heritage and the Market, Regulation and Desublimation'. In Dollimore and Sinfield, eds, *Political Shakespeare*, 255–79 (264).

44 Graham Holderness and Marcus Nevitt, 'Major Among the Minors: A Cultural Materialist Reading of *Julius Caesar*'. In *'Julius Caesar': New Critical Essays*, ed. Horst Zander (New York and London, 2005), 257–69.

45 Ibid., 259–64. Compulsory tests for fourteen-year-olds were eventually abandoned in 2008.

46 Sinfield, 'Heritage and the Market', 267. There is some pleasing evidence that this approach continues to be applied at GCSE level. In an essay published in 2003, Elaine Harris, Head of English at a comprehensive school in Harlow, quotes Sinfield on the fine distinction made in *Macbeth* between approved (state-authorized) violence and condemned (revolutionary) violence, and describes how she encourages eleven- to fourteen-year-olds to identify such instances in their analyses of the play. See Harris, 'New Town Shakespeare: A Comprehensive School Approach at Key Stages Three and Four', in *Shakespeare in Education*, 40–68 (49).

47 'John Hodgson interviewed by Christopher J. McCullough'. In *The Shakespeare Myth*, ed. Graham Holderness (Manchester, 1988), 160–5 (162, 163).

48 Ibid., 164–5.

49 'Michael Croft interviewed by Christopher J. McCullough'. In Holderness, ed., *The Shakespeare Myth*, 166–72 (169, 171–2).

50 Ibid., 167.

51 David Hornbrook, '"Go Play, Boy, Play": Shakespeare and Educational Drama'. In Holderness, ed., *The Shakespeare Myth*, 145–59 (149).

52 Ibid., 157.

53 Ann Thompson, '*King Lear* and the Politics of Teaching Shakespeare'. *Shakespeare Quarterly* 41 (1990): 139–46 (144).

54 Ibid., 146.

55 Sarah Olive, *Shakespeare Valued: Education Policy and Pedagogy 1989–2009* (Bristol, 2015), 41.

56 Ibid., 44.

57 Ibid., 132.

58 Jessica Shepherd, 'Michael Gove Labels Professors Critical of New Curriculum as "Bad Academia"'. *Guardian*, 21 March 2013. Online at https://www.theguardian.com/education/2013/mar/21/michael-gove-professors-new-national-curriculum (accessed 18 June 2016).

59 William Stewart, 'Gove's Curriculum Could Lead to Chaos, Leaders Warn'. *Times Educational Supplement*, 14 April 2013. Online at https://newteachers.tes.co.uk/content/gove's-curriculum-could-lead-chaos-leaders-war (accessed 18 June 2016).

60 A better-known example of Gove's anti-intellectualism occurred during a live TV debate during the 2016 Brexit campaign, when in response to a question about the paucity of economists who supported the UK's exit from the EU Gove replied 'people in this country have had enough of experts'. See Henry Mance, 'Britain Has Had Enough of Experts, Says Gove'. *Financial Times*, 3 June 2016. Online at http://www.ft.com/cms/s/0/3be49734-29cb-11e6-83e4-abc22d5d108c.html#axzz4EqjSdfgw (accessed 18 June 2016).

61 Dollimore, *Sexual Dissidence*, 89.

62 Extracts from these texts are appended to William Shakespeare, *The Tempest*, eds Virginia Mason Vaughan and Alden T. Vaughan (London, 1999), 287–314.

63 See ibid., 98–108.

64 See Stephen Greenblatt, 'Invisible Bullets: Renaissance Authority and its Subversion, *Henry IV* and *Henry V*'. In Dollimore and Sinfield, eds, *Political Shakespeare*, 18–47 (29). Greenblatt treated *The Tempest* at greater length in *Shakespearean Negotiations* (Berkeley and Los Angeles, 1988).

65 Vaughan and Vaughan, eds, *The Tempest*.

66 Paul Brown, '"This Thing of Darkness I Acknowledge Mine": *The Tempest* and the Discourse of Colonialism'. In Dollimore and Sinfield, eds, *Political Shakespeare*, 48–71 (68).

67 Ibid.

68 Ibid.

69 Francis Barker and Peter Hulme, 'Nymphs and Reapers Heavily Vanish: The Discursive Con-Texts of *The Tempest*'. In *Alternative Shakespeares*, ed. John Drakakis (London, 1985), 191–205 (204).

70 Ibid., 200.

71 Ibid., 203. Italics in original.

72 Ibid., 204.

73 Ania Loomba, *Shakespeare, Race and Colonialism* (Oxford, 2002), 164.

74 For a more detailed discussion of postcolonial rewritings of *The Tempest*, see Rob Nixon, 'Caribbean and African Appropriations of *The Tempest*'. *Critical Enquiry* 13 (1987): 557–78.

75 Loomba, *Shakespeare, Race and Colonialism*, 164.

76 Ania Loomba, *Gender, Race, Renaissance Drama* (Manchester, 1989), 143. Italics in original.

77 William Shakespeare, *The Tempest*, ed. Frank Kermode (London, 1954), xlii, quoted in Loomba, *Gender, Race, Renaissance Drama*, 143.

78 Scott Wilson, *Cultural Materialism: Theory and Practice* (Oxford, 1995), 8.

79 Ibid.

80 Loomba, *Gender, Race, Renaissance Drama*, 143.

81 Loomba, *Shakespeare, Race and Colonialism*, 165.

82 Ania Loomba, 'Shakespeare and Cultural Difference'. In *Alternative Shakespeares*, vol. 2, ed. Terence Hawkes (London, 1996), 164–91 (176).

83 William Shakespeare, *Antony and Cleopatra*, ed. John Wilders (London, 1995).

84 William Shakespeare, *Othello*, ed. E. A. J. Honigmann (London, 1997).

85 Loomba, *Shakespeare, Race and Colonialism*, 46.

86 Ibid., 81.

87 William Shakespeare, *Titus Andronicus*, ed. Jonathan Bate (London, 1995).

88 This is not to say that Aaron is straightforwardly villainous throughout the play. See Loomba, *Shakespeare, Race and Colonialism*, 75–90; Bate, ed., *Titus Andronicus*, 48–59; Jeannette S. White, '"Is Black So Base a Hue?" Shakespeare's Aaron and the Politics and Poetics of Race'. *CLA Journal* 40 (1997): 336–67 for full accounts of Aaron's character.

89 Loomba, *Shakespeare, Race and Colonialism*, 150. See also William Shakespeare, *The Merchant of Venice*, ed. John Drakakis (London, 2010), 17–40.

90 Loomba, 'Shakespeare and Cultural Difference', 190.

91 Loomba, *Shakespeare, Race and Colonialism*, 7.

92 Sinfield, *Shakespeare, Authority, Sexuality*, 27.

93 Dollimore, 'Introduction: Shakespeare, Cultural Materialism and the New Historicism'. In Dollimore and Sinfield, eds, *Political Shakespeare*, 2–17 (2–3).

94 The topic of Shakespeare and feminist theory is addressed by Marianne Novy in another volume in this series.

95 Kathleen McLuskie, 'The Patriarchal Bard: Feminist Criticism and Shakespeare: *King Lear* and *Measure for Measure*'. In

Dollimore and Sinfield, eds, *Political Shakespeare*, 88–108 (97–8).

96 See *OED* 1b and *The Winter's Tale*, ed. John Pitcher (London, 2014), 2.1.146–9 where Antigonus threatens to geld his three daughters.

97 McLuskie, 'The Patriarchal Bard', 98.

98 For a discussion of these issues see Catherine Belsey, 'Disrupting Sexual Difference: Meaning and Gender in the Comedies'. In Drakakis, ed., *Alternative Shakespeares*, 166–90; also Carol Thomas Neely, *Distracted Subjects: Madness and Gender in Shakespeare and Early Modern Culture* (Ithaca and London, 2004), 121–8.

99 McLuskie, 'The Patriarchal Bard', 106.

100 Boose is particularly critical of new historicists, pointing out that the non-literary texts they privilege 'are always and predictably male-authored'; see 'The Family in Shakespeare Studies; or – Studies in the Family of Shakespeareans; or – The Politics of Politics'. *Renaissance Quarterly* 40 (1987): 707–42 (732).

101 Ibid., 724. Other responses to McLuskie include Carol Thomas Neely, 'Constructing the Subject: Feminist Practice and the New Renaissance Discourses'. *English Literary Renaissance* 18 (1988): 5–18; Kiernan Ryan, *Shakespeare* (Hemel Hempstead, 1989).

102 Boose, 'The Family in Shakespeare Studies', 725–6.

103 Jonathan Dollimore, 'Shakespeare, Cultural Materialism, Feminism and Marxist Humanism'. *New Literary History* 21 (1990): 471–93 (475).

104 Ibid.

105 See Margaret Jane Kidnie, *Shakespeare and the Problem of Adaptation* (Oxford, 2009) and Rachel Carroll, ed., *Adaptation in Contemporary Culture: Textual Infidelities* (London, 2009).

106 Boose, 'The Family in Shakespeare Studies', 724.

107 Alan Sinfield, *Faultlines: Cultural Materialism and the Politics of Dissident Reading* (Oxford, 1992), 36.

108 Jonathan Dollimore, *Sex, Literature and Censorship* (Cambridge, 2001), 38.

109 Sinfield, *Shakespeare, Authority, Sexuality*, 198. Italics in original.

110 Kathleen McLuskie, *Renaissance Dramatists* (New Jersey, 1989), 229.

111 See *A Feminist Companion to Shakespeare*, ed. Dympna Callaghan, 2nd edn (Oxford, 2016).

112 Dollimore, 'Introduction: Shakespeare, Cultural Materialism and the New Historicism'. In Dollimore and Sinfield, eds, *Political Shakespeare*, 2–17 (11).

113 Sinfield, *Shakespeare, Authority, Sexuality*, 15.

114 On homosexuality, see Alan Bray, *Homosexuality in Renaissance England*, 2nd edn (London, 1988); Bruce R. Smith, *Homosexual Desire in Shakespeare's England: A Cultural Poetics* (Chicago, 1991). For a discussion of the competing claims of male friendship and marriage in the play, see Catherine Belsey, 'Love in Venice'. *Shakespeare Survey* 44 (1991): 41–53.

115 Sinfield, *Shakespeare, Authority, Sexuality*, 67.

116 Wilson, *Cultural Materialism*, 21.

117 Esther Newton and Shirley Walton, 'The Misunderstanding: Toward a More Precise Sexual Vocabulary'. In *Pleasure and Danger: Exploring Female Sexuality*, ed. Carole S. Vance (London, 1984), 242–50 (249–50), quoted in Sinfield, *Shakespeare, Authority, Sexuality*, 170.

Chapter 5

1 Jonathan Dollimore and Alan Sinfield, 'Foreword to the First Edition: Cultural Materialism'. In *Political Shakespeare: Essays in Cultural Materialism*, eds Jonathan Dollimore and Alan Sinfield, 2nd edn (Manchester, 1994), vii–viii (viii).

2 Boris Ford, 'Bardbiz', Letters. *The London Review of Books*, 2 August 1990, quoted in John Drakakis, '"Fashion it Thus": *Julius Caesar* and the Politics of Theatrical Representation'. In

Materialist Shakespeare: A History, ed. Ivo Kamps (London, 1995), 280–91 (289).

3 Terence Hawkes, *Meaning by Shakespeare* (London, 1992), 3. Italics in original.

4 Walter Benjamin, *Illuminations*, trans. Harry Zohn (London, 1973), 25–89.

5 Jonathan Dollimore, *Radical Tragedy: Religion, Ideology and Power in the Drama of Shakespeare and his Contemporaries*, reissued 3rd edn (Basingstoke, 2010), xxxi–xxxii.

6 Ibid., xxxiii.

7 Ibid., 198.

8 Jonathan Dollimore, *Sex, Literature and Censorship* (Cambridge, 2001), 132.

9 Ewan Fernie, 'Dollimore's Challenge'. *Shakespeare Studies* 35 (2007): 133–57 (153).

10 Dollimore, *Radical Tragedy*, xxxviii.

11 Donald J. Trump with Meredith McIver, *Think Like a Champion: An Informal Education in Business and Life* (New York, 2009), 107.

12 Alan Sinfield, 'Royal Shakespeare: Theatre and the Making of Ideology'. In Dollimore and Sinfield, eds, *Political Shakespeare*, 182–205 (185).

13 Alan Sinfield, *Faultlines: Cultural Materialism and the Politics of Dissident Reading* (Oxford, 1992), 14.

14 William Shakespeare, *Julius Caesar*, ed. David Daniell (London, 1998).

15 Andrew Hadfield, *Shakespeare and Republicanism* (Cambridge, 2005), 171.

16 Simon Barker, '"It's an Actor, Boss. Unarmed": The Rhetoric of *Julius Caesar*'. In *'Julius Caesar': New Critical Essays*, ed. Horst Zander (New York and London, 2005), 227–39 (239). Italics in original.

17 Drakakis, '"Fashion it Thus"', 289.

18 Graham Holderness and Marcus Nevitt, 'Major Among the Minors: A Cultural Materialist Reading of *Julius Caesar*'. In Zander, ed., *'Julius Caesar'*, 257–69 (264).

19 Sinfield, *Faultlines*, 19.

20 Ibid., 26.

21 Ronald B. Bond, ed., '*Certain Sermons or Homilies' (1547) and 'A Homily Against Disobedience and Wilful Rebellion' (1570): A Critical Edition* (Toronto, 1987), 211, 213.

22 Jonathan Dollimore, 'Introduction: Shakespeare, Cultural Materialism and the New Historicism'. In Dollimore and Sinfield, eds, *Political Shakespeare*, 2–17 (5).

23 Roger B. Manning, *Village Revolts: Social Protest and Popular Disturbances in England, 1509–1640* (Oxford, 1988), 312.

24 Harold Spencer Scott, ed., *The Journal of Sir Roger Wilbraham ... for the Years 1593–1616* (London, 1902), 92–4.

25 John Ponet, *A Short Treatise of Politic Power 1556* (Menston, 1970), G6v. Characters modernized.

26 Sinfield, *Faultlines*, 45.

27 Annabel Patterson, *Shakespeare and the Popular Voice* (Oxford, 1989), 11.

28 Coppélia Kahn, *Roman Shakespeare: Warriors, Wounds and Women* (London, 1997), 4.

29 See Patterson, *Shakespeare and the Popular Voice*, 32–51. For *Coriolanus*, see Patterson, *Shakespeare and the Popular Voice*, 120–53; Christopher Hill, *Change and Continuity in Seventeenth-Century England* (London, 1974), 185; Michael D. Bristol, 'Lenten Butchery: Legitimation Crisis in *Coriolanus*'. In *Shakespeare Reproduced: The Text in History and Ideology*, eds Jean E. Howard and Marion F. O'Connor (London, 1987), 207–24; for a contrary view, see Jerald W. Spotswood, '"We are Undone Already": Disarming the Multitude in *Julius Caesar* and *Coriolanus*'. *Texas Studies in Literature and Language* 42 (2000): 61–78.

30 Freyja Cox Jensen, *Reading the Roman Republic in Early Modern England* (Leiden and Boston, 2012), 151, quoting Suzanne F. Kistler, 'The Significance of the Missing Hero in Chapman's *Caesar and Pompey*'. *Modern Language Quarterly* 40 (1979): 339–57 (341).

31 Robert Miola, '*Julius Caesar* and the Tyrannicide Debate'. *Renaissance Quarterly* 38 (1985): 271–89 (273).

32 Ibid., 288.

33 Barbara L. Parker, '"A Thing Unfirm": Plato's *Republic* and Shakespeare's *Julius Caesar*'. *Shakespeare Quarterly* 44 (1993): 30–43 (38).

34 Ian Munro, *The Figure of the Crowd in Early Modern London: The City and its Double* (New York, 2005), 151.

35 Spotswood, '"We are Undone Already"', 62.

36 The festive character of shoemakers was established in print by Thomas Deloney's *The Gentle Craft* (1597) and confirmed by Thomas Dekker's *The Shoemakers' Holiday* (1599).

37 Tom Bishop, 'Shakespeare's Tragedy and Roman History'. In *The Oxford Handbook of Shakespearean Tragedy*, eds Michael Neill and David Schalkwyk (Oxford, 2016), 234–49 (243).

38 William Shakespeare, *Julius Caesar*, ed. David Daniell (London, 1998), 157.

39 Bate, 'The Cobbler's Awl: *Julius Caesar*, I.i.21–24'. *Shakespeare Quarterly* 35 (1984): 461–2; *Shakespeare's Sonnets*, ed. Stephen Booth (New Haven and London, 2000), 177. For 'meddle' and 'women's matters', see Eric Partridge, *Shakespeare's Bawdy* (London and New York, 2002), 190, 288.

40 There may be a connection here to the rumours of Julius Caesar's sexual liaisons with other men, as mentioned by Suetonius, Plutarch, Cicero and others. See, for example, Kelly Olson, 'Masculinity, Appearance and Sexuality: Dandies in Roman Antiquity'. *Journal of the History of Sexuality* 23 (2014): 182–205.

41 See Daniell, ed., *Julius Caesar*, 201.

42 See *OED* 2a.

43 Manning, *Village Revolts*, 309.

44 Holderness and Nevitt, 'Major Among the Minors', 266–7.

45 Naomi Conn Liebler, 'Buying and Selling So(u)les: Marketing Strategies and the Politics of Performance in *Julius Caesar*'. In Zander, ed., *'Julius Caesar'*, 165–79 (174).

46 Daniel Juan Gil, '"Bare Life": Political Order and the Specter of Antisocial Being in Shakespeare's *Julius Caesar*'. *Common Knowledge* 13 (2007): 67–79 (77–8).

47 For recent work on zombies see Edward P. Comentale and Aaron Jaffe, eds, *The Year's Work at the Zombie Research Center* (Indiana, 2014); Laura Hubner, Marcus Leaning and Paul Manning, eds, *The Zombie Renaissance in Popular Culture* (Basingstoke, 2015).

48 *Dawn of the Dead* (1978), [Film] Dir. George A. Romero, USA: United Film.

49 See Isaac Marion, *Warm Bodies* (London, 2010).

50 Laurie Rozakis, *Zombie Notes: A Study Guide to the Best in Undead Literary Classics* (Guildford, CT, 2009), 43.

51 Ibid., 58.

52 See James Shapiro, *Shakespeare and the Jews*, 20th anniversary edn (New York and Chichester, 2016), and William Shakespeare, *The Merchant of Venice*, ed. John Drakakis (London, 2011).

53 Jonathan Dollimore, *Sex, Literature and Censorship* (Cambridge, 2001), 157.

54 Roger Ebert, *Dawn of the Dead* Review, 4 May 1979. Online at http://www.rogerebert.com/reviews/dawn-of-the-dead-1979 (accessed 17 August 2016).

55 Jonathan Dollimore and Alan Sinfield, 'Culture and Textuality: Debating Cultural Materialism'. *Textual Practice* 4 (1990): 91–100 (92).

56 Peter Yeung, 'EU Referendum: Reports of Hate Crime Increase 57% following Brexit Vote'. *Independent*, 27 June 2016. Online at http://www.independent.co.uk/news/uk/home-news/brexit-hate-crime-racism-reports-eu-referendum-latest-a7106116.html (accessed 17 August 2016).

57 Footage of the full speech can be seen at https://www.youtube.com/watch?v=3ANT7sS3gWw, with the reference to *Julius Caesar* beginning around 50 seconds from the start.

58 Jon Stone, 'Boris Johnson Rules Himself out of Conservative Party Leadership Race in Surprise Announcement'. *Independent*, 30 June 2016. Online at http://www.independent.co.uk/news/uk/politics/boris-johnson-will-not-stand-for-tory-leader-he-announces-a7110921.html (accessed 18 August 2016).

59 Louis Althusser, *For Marx*, trans. Ben Brewster (London, 2005), 234.

60 The full speech can be read at http://www.telegraph.co.uk/news/2016/07/21/donald-trumps-leaked-republican-national-convention-speech-in-fu/ (accessed 18 August 2016).

61 Dollimore, *Radical Tragedy*, xxxviii.

62 Sinfield, *Faultlines*, 16–17.

63 Ibid., 25.

64 http://blog.shakespearesglobe.com/post/143888653268/word-by-word-the-complete-tweets-were-excited-to (accessed 18 August 2016).

BIBLIOGRAPHY

Althusser, Louis. 'Ideology and Ideological State Apparatuses'. In *Lenin and Philosophy and Other Essays*, trans. Ben Brewster. London: Monthly Review Press, 1971.

Althusser, Louis. *For Marx*, trans. Ben Brewster. London: Verso, 2005.

Armstrong, Isobel. 'Thatcher's Shakespeare?' *Textual Practice* 3 (1989): 1–13.

Bacon, Francis. *The Major Works*, ed. Brian Vickers. Oxford: Oxford University Press, 2002.

Barker, Francis and Peter Hulme. 'Nymphs and Reapers Heavily Vanish: The Discursive Con-Texts of *The Tempest*'. In *Alternative Shakespeares*, ed. John Drakakis, 191–205. London: Routledge, 1985.

Barker, Simon et al. 'Editorial'. *LTP: Journal of Literature Teaching Politics* 1 (1982): 1–3.

Barker, Simon. '"It's an Actor, Boss. Unarmed": The Rhetoric of *Julius Caesar*'. In *'Julius Caesar': New Critical Essays*, ed. Horst Zander, 227–39. New York and London: Routledge, 2005.

Bate, Jonathan. 'The Cobbler's Awl: *Julius Caesar*, I.i.21–24'. *Shakespeare Quarterly* 35 (1984): 461–2.

Bate, Jonathan. *The Genius of Shakespeare*. London: Picador, 1997.

Belsey, Catherine, 'Disrupting Sexual Difference: Meaning and Gender in the Comedies'. In *Alternative Shakespeares*, ed. John Drakakis, 166–90. London: Routledge, 1985.

Belsey, Catherine. *The Subject of Tragedy*. London: Routledge, 1985.

Belsey, Catherine. 'Towards Cultural History – in Theory and in Practice'. *Textual Practice* 3 (1989): 159–72.

Belsey, Catherine. 'Love in Venice'. *Shakespeare Survey* 44 (1991): 41–53.

Belsey, Catherine. 'Historicizing New Historicism'. In *Presentist Shakespeares*, eds Hugh Grady and Terence Hawkes, 27–45. London: Routledge, 2007.

Belsey, Catherine. *A Future for Criticism*. Oxford: Wiley-Blackwell, 2011.

Benjamin, Walter. *Illuminations*, trans. Harry Zohn. London: Fontana, 1973.

Bishop, Tom. 'Shakespeare's Tragedy and Roman History'. In *The Oxford Handbook of Shakespearean Tragedy*, eds Michael Neill and David Schalkwyk, 234–49. Oxford: Oxford University Press, 2016.

Blocksidge, Martin. 'Shakespeare: Iconic or Relevant?' In *Shakespeare in Education*, ed. Martin Blocksidge, 1–19. London: Bloomsbury, 2003.

Bond, Ronald B., ed. *'Certain Sermons or Homilies' (1547) and 'A Homily Against Disobedience and Wilful Rebellion' (1570): A Critical Edition*. Toronto: University of Toronto Press, 1987.

Boose, Lynda E. 'The Family in Shakespeare Studies; or – Studies in the Family of Shakespeareans; or – The Politics of Politics'. *Renaissance Quarterly* 40 (1987): 707–42.

Booth, Stephen, ed. *Shakespeare's Sonnets*. New Haven and London: Yale University Press, 2000.

Bray, Alan. 'Homosexuality and the Signs of Male Friendship in Elizabethan England'. In *Queering the Renaissance*, ed. Jonathan Goldberg, 40–61. Durham, NC: Duke University Press, 1994.

Bray, Alan. *Homosexuality in Renaissance England*, 2nd edn. London: Gay Men's Press, 1988.

Bray, Alan. *The Friend*. Chicago: Univeristy of Chicago Press, 2003.

Bristol, Michael. 'Lenten Butchery: Legitimation Crisis in *Coriolanus*'. In *Shakespeare Reproduced: The Text in History and Ideology*, eds Jean E. Howard and Marion F. O'Connor, 207–24. London: Routledge, 1987.

Bristol, Michael. *Big-Time Shakespeare*. London and New York: Routledge, 1996.

Brooks, Cleanth. 'The Formalist Critics'. *Kenyon Review* 13 (1951): 72–81 (72).

Brown, Paul. '"This Thing of Darkness I Acknowledge Mine": *The Tempest* and the Discourse of Colonialism'. In *Political Shakespeare: Essays in Cultural Materialism*, eds Jonathan Dollimore and Alan Sinfield, 2nd edn, 48–71. Manchester: Manchester University Press, 1994.

Bruster, Douglas. *Shakespeare and the Question of Culture: Early*

Modern Literature and the Cultural Turn. Basingstoke: Palgrave, 2003.

Callaghan, Dympna, ed. *A Feminist Companion to Shakespeare*, 2nd edn. Oxford: Wiley-Blackwell, 2016.

Carroll, Rachel, ed. *Adaptation in Contemporary Culture: Textual Infidelities*. London: Continuum, 2009.

Cavanagh, Dermot. 'The Language of Treason in *Richard II*'. *Shakespeare Studies* 27 (1999): 134–60.

Collini, Stefan. *What are Universities For?* London: Penguin, 2012.

Comentale, Edward P. and Aaron Jaffe, eds. *The Year's Work at the Zombie Research Center*. Bloomington: Indiana University Press, 2014.

Copenhaver, Brian P. and Charles B. Schmitt. *Renaissance Philosophy*. Oxford: Oxford University Press, 1992.

Derrida, Jacques. *Positions*, trans. Alan Bass. Chicago: University of Chicago Press, 1971.

Derrida, Jacques. *Margins of Philosophy*, trans. Alan Bass. Chicago and London: University of Chicago Press, 1982.

DiPietro, Cary and Hugh Grady. 'Introduction'. In *Shakespeare and the Urgency of Now: Criticism and Theory in the 21st Century*, eds Cary DiPietro and Hugh Grady, 1–8. Basingstoke: Palgrave Macmillan, 2013.

Dollimore, Jonathan. 'Shakespeare, Cultural Materialism, Feminism and Marxist Humanism'. *New Literary History* 21 (1990): 471–93.

Dollimore, Jonathan. *Sexual Dissidence: Augustine to Wilde, Freud to Foucault*. Oxford: Oxford University Press, 1991.

Dollimore, Jonathan. 'Introduction: Shakespeare, Cultural Materialism and the New Historicism'. In *Political Shakespeare: Essays in Cultural Materialism*, eds Jonathan Dollimore and Alan Sinfield, 2nd edn, 2–17. Manchester: Manchester University Press, 1994.

Dollimore, Jonathan. *Sex, Literature and Censorship*. Cambridge: Polity, 2001.

Dollimore, Jonathan. *Radical Tragedy: Religion, Ideology and Power in the Drama of Shakespeare and his Contemporaries*, rev. 3rd edn. Basingstoke: Palgrave Macmillan, 2010.

Dollimore, Jonathan. 'The Legacy of Cultural Materialism'. *Textual Practice* 27 (2013): 715–24.

Dollimore, Jonathan. 'A Response to Neema Parvini'. *Textual Practice* 27 (2013): 733–5.

Dollimore, Jonathan. 'Then and Now'. *Critical Survey* 26 (2014): 61–82.

Dollimore, Jonathan and David Jonathan Y. Bayot. *Jonathan Dollimore in Conversation*. Manila: De La Salle University Publishing House, 2013.

Dollimore, Jonathan and Alan Sinfield. 'History and Ideology: The Instance of *Henry V*.' In *Alternative Shakespeares*, ed. John Drakakis, 206–27. London: Routledge, 1985.

Dollimore, Jonathan and Alan Sinfield. 'Culture and Textuality: Debating Cultural Materialism'. *Textual Practice* 4 (1990): 91–100.

Dollimore, Jonathan and Alan Sinfield. 'Foreword to the First Edition: Cultural Materialism'. In *Political Shakespeare: Essays in Cultural Materialism*, eds Jonathan Dollimore and Alan Sinfield, 2nd edn, vii–viii. Manchester: Manchester University Press, 1994.

Donne, John. *The Major Works*, ed. John Carey. Oxford: Oxford University Press, 1990.

Drakakis, John. 'Terminator 2½: Or Messing with Canons'. *Textual Practice* 7 (1993): 60–84.

Drakakis, John. '"Fashion it Thus": *Julius Caesar* and the Politics of Theatrical Representation'. In *Materialist Shakespeare: A History*, ed. Ivo Kamps, 280–91. London: Verso, 1995.

Drakakis, John. 'Afterword: The Next Generation'. In *Alternative Shakespeares*, vol. 2, ed. Terence Hawkes, 238–44. London: Routledge, 1996.

Drakakis, John. 'Cultural Materialism'. In *The Cambridge History of Literary Criticism, Vol. IX: Twentieth-Century Historical, Philosophical and Psychological Perspectives*, eds Christa Knellwolf and Christopher Norris, 43–58. Cambridge: Cambridge University Press, 2001.

Dreyfus, Hubert L. and Paul Rabinow. *Michel Foucault: Beyond Structuralism and Hermeneutics*. Brighton: Harvester, 1982.

Dunn, Esther Cloudman. *Shakespeare in America*. New York: Macmillan, 1939.

Eagleton, Terry. *The Function of Criticism: From 'The Spectator' to Post-Structuralism*. London: Verso, 1984.

Eagleton, Terry. *Literary Theory: An Introduction*, 2nd edn. Oxford: Blackwell, 1996.

Ebert, Roger. *Dawn of the Dead* Review, 4 May 1979. Available

online: http://www.rogerebert.com/reviews/dawn-of-
the-dead-1979 (accessed 15 December 2016).

Egan, Gabriel. *Shakespeare and Marx*. Oxford: Oxford University
Press, 2004.

Elyot, Thomas. *The Book Named the Governor*, ed. S. E.
Lehmberg. London: Dent, 1962.

Fernie, Ewan. 'Dollimore's Challenge'. *Shakespeare Studies* 35
(2007): 133–57.

Ford, Boris. 'Bardbiz'. Letters in *The London Review of Books*,
2 August 1990.

Foucault, Michel. *The Order of Things: An Archaeology of the
Human Sciences*. London: Routledge, 1970.

Foucault, Michel, *Power/Knowledge: Selected Interviews and Other
Writings 1972–1977*, ed. Colin Gordon, trans. Colin Gordon et
al. Hemel Hempstead: Harvester Wheatsheaf, 1980.

Foucault, Michel. *The History of Sexuality Volume I: An
Introduction*, trans. Robert Hurley. London: Penguin, 1981.

Frey, Charles H. *Experiencing Shakespeare: Essays on Text,
Classroom, and Performance*. Columbia: University of Missouri
Press, 1988.

Gajowski, Evelyn. 'The Presence of the Past'. In *Presentism, Gender
and Sexuality in Shakespeare*, ed. Evelyn Gajowski, 1–22.
Basingstoke: Palgrave Macmillan, 2009.

Gallagher, Catherine and Stephen Greenblatt. *Practicing New
Historicism*. Chicago: University of Chicago Press, 2000.

Gil, Daniel Juan, '"Bare Life": Political Order and the Specter
of Antisocial Being in Shakespeare's *Julius Caesar*'. *Common
Knowledge* 13 (2007): 67–79.

Goulden, Holly and John Hartley. 'Nor Should Such
Topics as Homosexuality, Masturbation, Frigidity,
Premature Ejaculation or the Menopause be Regarded as
Unmentionable'. *LTP: Journal of Literature Teaching Politics*
1 (1982): 4–20.

Grady, Hugh. 'Shakespeare Studies, 2005: A Situated Overview'.
Shakespeare 1 (2005): 102–20.

Grady, Hugh and Terence Hawkes. 'Presenting Presentism'. In
Presentist Shakespeares, eds Hugh Grady and Terence Hawkes,
1–5. London and New York: Routledge, 2007.

Grayling, A. C. *Friendship*. New Haven and London: Yale
University Press, 2013.

Greenblatt, Stephen. *Renaissance Self-Fashioning: From More to Shakespeare*. Chicago: University of Chicago Press, 1980.

Greenblatt, Stephen. *Shakespearean Negotiations*. Berkeley and Los Angeles: University of California Press, 1988.

Greenblatt, Stephen. *Learning to Curse: Essays in Early Modern Culture*. New York and London: Routledge, 1990.

Greenblatt, Stephen. 'Invisible Bullets: Renaissance Authority and its Subversion, *Henry IV* and *Henry V*'. In *Political Shakespeare: Essays in Cultural Materialism*, eds Jonathan Dollimore and Alan Sinfield, 2nd edn, 18–47. Manchester: Manchester University Press, 1994.

Hadfield, Andrew. *Shakespeare and Republicanism*. Cambridge: Cambridge University Press, 2005.

Harris, Elaine. 'New Town Shakespeare: A Comprehensive School Approach at Key Stages Three and Four'. In *Shakespeare in Education*, ed. Martin Blocksidge, 40–68. London: Continuum, 2003.

Harris, Jonathan Gil. 'The New New Historicism's *Wunderkammer* of Objects'. *European Journal of English Studies* 4 (2000): 111–23.

Harris, Jonathan Gil. *Untimely Matter in the Time of Shakespeare*. Pennsylvania: University of Pennsylvania Press, 2009.

Hawkes, Terence. *That Shakespeherian Rag*. London and New York: Routledge, 1986.

Hawkes, Terence. *Meaning by Shakespeare*. London and New York: Routledge, 1992.

Hawthorn, Jeremy. *Cunning Passages: New Historicism, Cultural Materialism and Marxism in the Contemporary Debate*. London: Arnold, 1996.

Heinemann, Margot. 'How Brecht Read Shakespeare'. In *Political Shakespeare: Essays in Cultural Materialism*, eds Jonathan Dollimore and Alan Sinfield, 2nd edn, 226–54. Manchester: Manchester University Press, 1994.

Higgins, John. *Raymond Williams: Literature, Marxism and Cultural Materialism*. Oxford: Routledge, 1999.

Hill, Christopher. *Change and Continuity in Seventeenth-Century England*. London: Weidenfeld and Nicolson, 1974.

Holderness, Graham. *Cultural Shakespeare: Essays in the Shakespeare Myth*. Hatfield: University of Hertfordshire Press, 2001.

Holderness, Graham and Marcus Nevitt. 'Major Among the

Minors: A Cultural Materialist Reading of *Julius Caesar*'. In
'Julius Caesar': New Critical Essays, ed. Horst Zander, 257–69.
New York and London: Routledge, 2005.

Hornbrook, David. '"Go Play, Boy, Play": Shakespeare and
Educational Drama'. In *The Shakespeare Myth*, ed. Graham
Holderness, 145–59. Manchester: Manchester University Press,
1988.

Hubner, Laura, Marcus Leaning and Paul Manning, eds. *The
Zombie Renaissance in Popular Culture*. Basingstoke: Palgrave
Macmillan, 2015.

Jensen, Freyja Cox. *Reading the Roman Republic in Early Modern
England*. Leiden and Boston: Brill, 2012.

Johnson, Keith. *Shakespeare's English: A Practical Linguistic Guide*.
London: Routledge, 2013.

Joyce, James. *Ulysses*. London: Penguin, 1992.

Kahn, Coppélia. *Roman Shakespeare: Warriors, Wounds and
Women*. London: Routledge, 1997.

Kastan, David Scott. *Shakespeare after Theory*. New York and
London: University of Chicago Press, 1999.

Kelly, Joan. *Women, History and Theory*. Chicago: University of
Chicago Press, 1986.

Kidnie, Margaret Jane. *Shakespeare and the Problem of
Adaptation*. Oxford: Routledge, 2009.

Kistler, Suzanne F. 'The Significance of the Missing Hero in
Chapman's *Caesar and Pompey*'. *Modern Language Quarterly*
40 (1979): 339–57.

Kittredge, G. L., ed. *The Complete Works of Shakespeare*. Boston:
Ginn, MA, 1936.

Kurtz, Paul, ed. *The Humanist Alternative*. London: Prometheus, 1973.

Levy, Eric P. *Hamlet and the Rethinking of Man*. Madison:
Fairleigh Dickinson University Press, 2008.

Liebler, Naomi Conn. 'Buying and Selling So(u)les: Marketing
Strategies and the Politics of Performance in Julius Caesar'. In
'Julius Caesar': New Critical Essays, ed. Horst Zander, 165–79.
New York and London: Routledge, 2005.

Loomba, Ania. *Gender, Race, Renaissance Drama*. Manchester:
Manchester University Press, 1989.

Loomba, Ania. 'Shakespeare and Cultural Difference'. In
Alternative Shakespeares, vol. 2, ed. Terence Hawkes, 164–91.
London: Routledge, 1996.

Loomba, Ania. *Shakespeare, Race and Colonialism*. Oxford: Oxford University Press, 2002.

Macaulay, G. C., ed. *The Complete Works of John Gower*, 4 vols. Oxford: Early English Text Society, 1901.

Macherey, Pierre. *A Theory of Literary Production*, trans. Geoffrey Wall. London: Routledge, 2006.

Mance, Henry. 'Britain Has Had Enough of Experts, Says Gove', *Financial Times*, 3 June 2016. Available online: http://www.ft.com/cms/s/0/3be49734-29cb-11e6-83e4-abc22d5d108c.html#axzz4EqjSdfgw (accessed 16 December 2016).

Mandel, Ernest. 'Introduction'. In Karl Marx, *Capital: A Critique of Political Economy*, trans. Ben Fowkes, 11–86, vol. 1. London: Penguin, 1976.

Manning, Roger B. *Village Revolts: Social Protest and Popular Disturbances in England, 1509–1640*. Oxford: Clarendon Press, 1988.

Marion, Isaac. *Warm Bodies*. London: Vintage Press, 2010.

Marlow, Christopher. *Performing Masculinity in English University Drama, 1598–1636*. Farnham: Ashgate, 2013.

Marx, Karl. *Capital: A Critique of Political Economy*, vol. 1, trans. Ben Fowkes. London: Penguin, 1976.

Marx, Karl. *The Eighteenth Brumaire of Louis Bonaparte*. Moscow: Progress, 1934.

Marx, Karl. *Selected Writings in Sociology and Social Philosophy*, eds T. B. Bottomore and Maximilien Rubel. Harmondsworth: Penguin, 1963.

Marx, Karl and Friedrich Engels. *The Communist Manifesto*, trans. Samuel Moore. London: Penguin, 1967.

McCullough, Christopher J. 'John Hodgson Interviewed by Christopher J. McCullough'. In *The Shakespeare Myth*, ed. Graham Holderness, 160–5. Manchester: Manchester University Press, 1988.

McCullough, Christopher J. 'Michael Croft Interviewed by Christopher J. McCullough'. In *The Shakespeare Myth*, ed. Graham Holderness, 166–72. Manchester: Manchester University Press, 1988.

McGettigan, Andrew. *The Great University Gamble: Money, Markets and the Future of Higher Education*. London: Pluto, 2013.

McLuskie, Kathleen. 'The Patriarchal Bard: Feminist Criticism and Shakespeare: *King Lear* and *Measure for Measure*'. In *Political*

Shakespeare: Essays in Cultural Materialism, eds Jonathan Dollimore and Alan Sinfield, 2nd edn, 88–108. Manchester: Manchester University Press, 1994.

McLuskie, Kathleen. *Renaissance Dramatists*. Atlantic Highlands, NJ: Humanities Press International, 1989.

Milner, Andrew. *Re-Imagining Cultural Studies: The Promise of Cultural Materialism*. London: Sage, 2002.

Miola, Robert. '*Julius Caesar* and the Tyrannicide Debate'. *Renaissance Quarterly* 38 (1985): 271–89.

Montrose, Louis Adrian. '"Shaping Fantasies": Figurations of Gender and Power in Elizabethan Culture'. *Representations* 2 (1983): 61–94.

Montrose, Louis Adrian. 'Professing the Renaissance: The Poetics and Politics of Culture'. In *The New Historicism*, ed. H. Aram Veeser, 15–36. New York and London: Routledge, 1989.

Mullaney, Steven. *The Place of the Stage: License, Play and Power in Renaissance England*. Chicago and London: University of Chicago Press, 1988.

Munro, Ian. *The Figure of the Crowd in Early Modern London: The City and its Double*. New York: Palgrave Macmillan, 2005.

Munro, Lucy. 'Shakespeare and the Uses of the Past: Critical Approaches and Current Debates'. *Shakespeare* 7 (2011): 102–25.

Neely, Carol Thomas. 'Constructing the Subject: Feminist Practice and the New Renaissance Discourses'. *English Literary Renaissance* 18 (1988): 5–18.

Neely, Carol Thomas. *Distracted Subjects: Madness and Gender in Shakespeare and Early Modern Culture*. Ithaca and London: Cornell University Press, 2004.

Newton, Esther and Shirley Walton. 'The Misunderstanding: Toward a More Precise Sexual Vocabulary'. In *Pleasure and Danger: Exploring Female Sexuality*, ed. Carole S. Vance, 242–50. London: Pandora, 1984.

Nixon, Rob. 'Caribbean and African Appropriations of *The Tempest*'. *Critical Enquiry* 13 (1987): 557–78.

Olive, Sarah. *Shakespeare Valued: Education Policy and Pedagogy 1989–2009*. Bristol: Intellect, 2015.

Olson, Kelly. 'Masculinity, Appearance and Sexuality: Dandies in Roman Antiquity'. *Journal of the History of Sexuality* 23 (2014): 182–205.

Parker, Barbara L. '"A Thing Unfirm": Plato's *Republic* and Shakespeare's *Julius Caesar*'. *Shakespeare Quarterly* 44 (1993): 30–43.

Partridge, Eric. *Shakespeare's Bawdy*. London and New York: Routledge, 2002.

Parvini, Neema. *Shakespeare and Contemporary Theory: New Historicism and Cultural Materialism*. London: Bloomsbury, 2012.

Parvini, Neema. *Shakespeare's History Plays: Rethinking Historicism*. Edinburgh: Edinburgh University Press, 2012.

Parvini, Neema. 'Reply to Jonathan Dollimore'. *Textual Practice* 27 (2013): 724–33.

Parvini, Neema. *Shakespeare and Cognition: Thinking Fast and Slow through Character*. Basingstoke: Palgrave Macmillan, 2015.

Patterson, Annabel. *Shakespeare and the Popular Voice*. Oxford: Blackwell, 1989.

Peacham, Thomas. *The Compleat Gentleman*. Oxford: Clarendon Press, 1906.

Pechter, Edward. *What Was Shakespeare? Renaissance Plays and Changing Critical Practice*. Ithaca: Cornwell University Press, 1995.

Pickett, Brent L. 'Foucault and the Politics of Resistance'. *Polity* 28 (1996): 445–66.

Ponet, John. *A Short Treatise of Politic Power 1556*. Menston: Scolar, 1970.

Porter, Carolyn. 'Are We Being Historical Yet?' *South Atlantic Quarterly* 87 (1988): 743–86.

Romero, George A., dir. *Dawn of the Dead* (1978) [Film] USA: United Film.

Rozakis, Laurie. *Zombie Notes: A Study Guide to the Best in Undead Literary Classics*. Guildford, CT: Lyons, 2009.

Ryan, Kiernan. *Shakespeare*. Hemel Hempstead: Harvester Wheatsheaf, 1989.

Ryan, Kiernan. *New Historicism and Cultural Materialism: A Reader*. London: Arnold, 1996.

Sartre, Jean-Paul. *Existentialism and Humanism*, trans. Philip Mairet. London: Methuen, 2007.

Scott, Harold Spencer, ed. *The Journal of Sir Roger Wilbraham … for the Years 1593–1616*. London: Royal Historical Society, 1902.

Shakespeare, William. *The Tempest*, ed. Frank Kermode. London: Methuen, 1954.

Shakespeare, William. *Hamlet*, ed. Harold Jenkins. London:
  Methuen, 1982.
Shakespeare, William. *Antony and Cleopatra*, ed. John Wilders.
  London: Routledge, 1995.
Shakespeare, William. *King Henry V*, ed. T. W. Craik. London:
  Methuen, 1995.
Shakespeare, William. *Titus Andronicus*, ed. Jonathan Bate.
  London: Routledge, 1995.
Shakespeare, William. *King Lear*, ed. R. A. Foakes. London:
  Thomas Nelson, 1997.
Shakespeare, William. *Othello*, ed. E. A. J. Honigmann. London:
  Thomas Nelson, 1997.
Shakespeare, William. *Julius Caesar*, ed. David Daniell. London:
  Thomas Nelson, 1998.
Shakespeare, William. *Troilus and Cressida*, ed. David Bevington.
  London: Thomas Nelson, 1998.
Shakespeare, William. *The Tempest*, ed. Virginia Mason Vaughan
  and Alden T. Vaughan. London: Thomas Nelson, 1999.
Shakespeare, William. *King Henry IV, Part 1*, ed. David Scott
  Kastan. London: Thomson Learning, 2002.
Shakespeare, William. *King Richard II*, ed. Charles R. Forker.
  London: Thomson Learning, 2002.
Shakespeare, William. *Pericles*, ed. Suzanne Gossett. London:
  Thomson Learning, 2004.
Shakespeare, William. *The Complete Works*, ed. John Jowett et al.,
  2nd edn. Oxford: Oxford University Press, 2005.
Shakespeare, William. *As You Like It*, ed. Juliet Dusinberre.
  London: Thomson Learning, 2006.
Shakespeare, William. *Hamlet*, eds Ann Thompson and Neil Taylor.
  London: Thomson Learning, 2006.
Shakespeare, William. *King Richard III*, ed. James R. Siemon.
  London: Methuen, 2009.
Shakespeare, William. *The Taming of the Shrew*, ed. Barbara
  Hodgdon. London: Methuen, 2010.
Shakespeare, William. *The Merchant of Venice*, ed. John Drakakis.
  London: Bloomsbury, 2011.
Shakespeare, William. *The Winter's Tale*, ed. John Pitcher. London:
  Bloomsbury, 2014.
Shakespeare, William. *Macbeth*, eds Sandra Clark and Pamela
  Mason. London: Bloomsbury, 2015.

Shapiro, James. *Shakespeare and the Jews*, 20th anniversary edn.
    New York and Chichester: Columbia University Press, 2016.
Shepherd, Jessica. 'Michael Gove Labels Professors Critical of New
    Curriculum as "Bad Academia"'. *Guardian*, 21 March 2013.
    Available online: https://www.theguardian.com/education/2013/
    mar/21/michael-gove-professors-new-national-curriculum
    (accessed 16 December 2016).
Sher, Anthony and Gregory Doran. *Woza Shakespeare: Titus
    Andronicus in South Africa*. London: Methuen, 1996.
Sinfield, Alan. 'Four Ways with a Reactionary Text'. *LTP: Journal
    of Literature Teaching Politics* 2 (1983): 81–95.
Sinfield, Alan. *Faultlines: Cultural Materialism and the Politics of
    Dissident Reading*. Oxford: Oxford University Press, 1992.
Sinfield, Alan. 'Introduction: Reproductions, Interventions'. In
    Political Shakespeare: Essays in Cultural Materialism, eds Jonathan
    Dollimore and Alan Sinfield, 2nd edn, 154–7. Manchester:
    Manchester University Press, 1994.
Sinfield, Alan. 'Give an Account of Shakespeare and Education,
    Showing Why You Think They are Effective and What You
    Have Appreciated About Them. Support Your Comments with
    Precise References'. In *Political Shakespeare: Essays in Cultural
    Materialism*, eds Jonathan Dollimore and Alan Sinfield, 2nd edn,
    158–81. Manchester: Manchester University Press, 1994.
Sinfield, Alan. 'Royal Shakespeare: Theatre and the Making
    of Ideology'. In *Political Shakespeare: Essays in Cultural
    Materialism*, eds Jonathan Dollimore and Alan Sinfield, 2nd edn,
    185–205. Manchester: Manchester University Press, 1994.
Sinfield, Alan. 'Heritage and the Market, Regulation and
    Desublimation'. In *Political Shakespeare: Essays in Cultural
    Materialism*, eds Jonathan Dollimore and Alan Sinfield, 2nd edn,
    255–79. Manchester: Manchester University Press, 1994.
Sinfield, Alan. 'How to Read *The Merchant of Venice* Without
    Being Heterosexist'. In *Alternative Shakespeares*, vol. 2, ed.
    Terence Hawkes, 122–39. London: Routledge, 1996.
Sinfield, Alan. *Cultural Politics – Queer Reading*, 2nd edn. London:
    Routledge, 2005.
Sinfield, Alan. *Shakespeare, Authority, Sexuality: Unfinished
    Business in Cultural Materialism*. Oxford: Routledge, 2006.
Smith, Bruce R. *Homosexual Desire in Shakespeare's England: A
    Cultural Poetics*. Chicago: University of Chicago Press, 1991.

Soper, Kate. *Humanism and Anti-Humanism*. London: Hutchinson, 1986.

Spivak, Gayatri Chakravorty. *In Other Worlds: Essays in Cultural Politics*. London and New York: Methuen, 1987.

Spotswood, Jerald W. '"We are Undone Already": Disarming the Multitude in *Julius Caesar* and *Coriolanus*'. *Texas Studies in Literature and Language* 42 (2000): 61–78.

Stewart, William. 'Gove's Curriculum Could Lead to Chaos, Leaders Warn'. *Times Educational Supplement*, 14 April 2013. Available online: https://www.tes.com/news/tes-archive/tes-publication/goves-curriculum-could-be-chaos-leaders-warn (accessed 15 December 2016).

Stone, Jon. 'Boris Johnson Rules Himself Out of Conservative Party Leadership Race in Surprise Announcement'. *Independent*, 30 June 2016. Available online: http://www.independent.co.uk/news/uk/politics/boris-johnson-will-not-stand-for-tory-leader-he-announces-a7110921.html (accessed 16 December 2016).

Swetnam, Joseph. *An Arraignment of Lewd, Idle, Froward and Unconstant Women*. London: Edw. Allde for Thomas Archer, 1615.

Taylor, Helen. '"Are We Talking about Literature?" A History of LTP'. *LTP: Journal of Literature Teaching Politics* 6 (1987): 7–12.

Taylor, Helen. 'Leaving Parties and Legacies: Reflections across the Binary Divide on a Decade of Englishes'. In *The State of Theory*, ed. Richard Bradford, 42–56. London: Routledge, 1993.

Thompson, Ann. '*King Lear* and the Politics of Teaching Shakespeare'. *Shakespeare Quarterly* 41 (1990): 139–46.

Tillyard, E. M. W. *The Elizabethan World Picture*. Harmondsworth: Penguin, 1943.

Tillyard, E. M. W. *Shakespeare's History Plays*. Harmondsworth: Penguin, 1944.

Trump, Donald J. with Meredith McIver. *Think Like a Champion: An Informal Education in Business and Life*. New York: Vanguard, 2009.

Wayne, Don E. 'Power, Politics and the Shakespearean Text: Recent Criticism in England and the United States'. In *Shakespeare Reproduced: The Text in History and Ideology*, eds Jean E. Howard and Marion F. O'Connor, 47–57. New York and London: Routledge, 1987.

Webster, John. *The Duchess of Malfi*, ed. Leah S. Marcus. London: Methuen, 2009.

White, Jeannette S. '"Is Black So Base a Hue?" Shakespeare's Aaron and the Politics and Poetics of Race'. *CLA Journal* 40 (1997): 336–67.

Williams, Raymond. *Marxism and Literature*. Oxford: Oxford University Press, 1977.

Williams, Raymond. *Politics and Letters: Interviews with New Left Review*. London: New Left Books, 1979.

Williams, Raymond. 'Notes on Marxism in Britain Since 1945'. In *Culture and Materialism: Selected Essays*, 233–51 (243). London: Verso, 1980.

Williams, Raymond. *Culture*. Glasgow: Collins, 1981.

Williams, Raymond. *Keywords: A Vocabulary of Culture and Society*, 2nd edn. London: Fontana, 1983.

Wilson Knight, G. *The Wheel of Fire: Interpretations of Shakespearian Tragedy*, 4th edn. London and New York: Routledge, 2001.

Wilson, Scott. *Cultural Materialism: Theory and Practice*. Oxford: Blackwell, 1995.

Yeung, Peter. 'EU Referendum: Reports of Hate Crime Increase 57% following Brexit Vote'. *Independent*, 27 June 2016. Available online: http://www.independent.co.uk/news/uk/home-news/brexit-hate-crime-racism-reports-eu-referendum-latest-a7106116.html (accessed 15 December 2016).

Online resources

http://blog.shakespearesglobe.com/post/143888653268/word-by-word-the-complete-tweets-were-excited-to

http://gamebookadventures.com/gamebooks/to-be-or-not-to-be/

http://www.goodreads.com/about/us

https://www.goodreads.com/author/quotes/947.William_Shakespeare

http://www.telegraph.co.uk/news/2016/07/21/donald-trumps-leaked-republican-national-convention-speech-in-fu/

https://www.youtube.com/watch?v=3ANT7sS3gWw

INDEX

Lightning Source UK Ltd.
Milton Keynes UK
UKHW041159250219
337970UK00005B/247/P

9 781472 572936